Fire Magic

Secrets of Witchcraft, Spells, Candle Burning Rituals, Norse Paganism, and Divination

© Copyright 2022

The content contained within this book may not be reproduced, duplicated, or transmitted without direct written permission from the author or the publisher.

Under no circumstances will any blame or legal responsibility be held against the publisher, or author, for any damages, reparation, or monetary loss due to the information contained within this book, either directly or indirectly.

Legal Notice:

This book is copyright protected. It is only for personal use. You cannot amend, distribute, sell, use, quote or paraphrase any part, or the content within this book, without the consent of the author or publisher.

Disclaimer Notice:

Please note the information contained within this document is for educational and entertainment purposes only. All effort has been executed to present accurate, up-to-date, reliable, complete information. No warranties of any kind are declared or implied. Readers acknowledge that the author is not engaging in the rendering of legal, financial, medical, or professional advice. The content within this book has been derived from various sources. Please consult a licensed professional before attempting any techniques outlined in this book.

By reading this document, the reader agrees that under no circumstances is the author responsible for any losses, direct or indirect, that are incurred as a result of the use of information contained within this document, including, but not limited to, errors, omissions, or inaccuracies.

Your Free Gift (only available for a limited time)

Thanks for getting this book! If you want to learn more about various spirituality topics, then join Mari Silva's community and get a free guided meditation MP3 for awakening your third eye. This guided meditation mp3 is designed to open and strengthen ones third eye so you can experience a higher state of consciousness. Simply visit the link below the image to get started.

https://spiritualityspot.com/meditation

Contents

INTRODUCTION 1
CHAPTER 1: WHAT IS FIRE MAGIC? 4
    THE HISTORY OF FIRE MAGIC 4
    FIRE AND OTHER ELEMENTS 6
    THE ROLE OF FIRE MAGIC AND RITUALS 7
    THE ANCIENT ART OF PYROMANCY 9
    CHARACTERISTICS AND SYMBOLIZATION OF FIRE 10
CHAPTER 2: FIRE ENTITIES – DRAGONS, DEITIES, AND ELEMENTALS 15
    MYTHICAL CREATURES 15
    CELTIC DEITIES 21
    GREEK DEITIES 23
    ROMAN DEITIES 24
    THE ROLE OF DRAGONS IN FIRE MAGIC 26
CHAPTER 3: SETTING UP A FIRE ALTAR SAFELY 28
    BUILDING A FIRE ALTER 28
    WHAT CAN THE FIRE ALTER BE USED FOR? 29
    FIRE OFFERINGS AND THEIR USES 29
    INCENSE BURNERS 29
    WHAT ABOUT LARGE CAULDRONS? 30
    THE IMPORTANCE OF AN ALTAR 30

    Tools and How to Use Them 31
    How to Maintain an Altar 35

CHAPTER 4: FIRE CRYSTALS, PLANTS, AND HERBS 37

    Fire Crystals 38
    The Healing Properties of Fire Crystals 38
    Crystals That Channel Fire Element Energy 39
    Fire Plants and Herbs 46
    Attributes of Fiery Herbs and Plants 47
    Fire Element Herbs 48
    Don't Forget About Fire Safety! 59

CHAPTER 5: FIRE AND NORSE MYTHS 60

    The Norse God of Trickery – Loki 61
    The Giant of Fire and Lava – Surtr 62
    The Giant of Fire – Logi 64
    God of Knowledge – Odin 65
    Fire of Hope – Balder 66
    The Norse Realm of Fire – Muspelheim 67

CHAPTER 6: CANDLE BURNING RITUALS 69

    Purpose of Candle Burning Rituals/Magic 69
    What You Need to Perform Candle Rituals 70
    How to Perform a Candle Ritual 71

CHAPTER 7: PAGAN FIRE FESTIVALS 79

    Beltane 80
    Candlemas 80
    Samhain 81
    Lughnasadh 82
    Imbolc 82
    Mabon 83
    Yule 83
    Wiccan Samhain Celebration 84
    Modern Parallels 84

CHAPTER 8: PERFORMING FIRE SPELLS SAFELY 91

    Fire Safety Tips You Should Know 91
    Other Safe Methods of Performing Fire Spells 96

SAFE FIRE SPELLS 98
CHAPTER 9: PYROMANCY – DIVINATION BY FIRE 100
WHAT IS PYROMANCY? 100
ALTERNATIVE APPROACHES TO PYROMANCY 102
PRACTICAL FORMS OF PYROMANCY 104
CHAPTER 10: YOUR OWN FIRE MAGIC RITUAL 108
FIRE RITUALS 109
CREATE YOUR OWN 113
DISCLAIMERS 116
CONCLUSION 118
HERE'S ANOTHER BOOK BY MARI SILVA THAT YOU MIGHT LIKE 120
YOUR FREE GIFT (ONLY AVAILABLE FOR A LIMITED TIME) 121
REFERENCES 122

Introduction

The element of fire plays an integral role in our daily lives. It is used for cooking, heating water, keeping us warm, and giving comfort. We use fire in various forms—bonfires, candles, and cooking stoves. Among all four significant elements necessary for existence, fire is probably the most intriguing and creative element of all. Fire symbolizes creativity, determination, passion, zeal, and compulsion. It drives a person to achieve their goals and become more focused in life. It acts as an inner light that guides us toward our main destination. If you feel lost or are stuck at a dead-end, peek into your soul to find your guiding fire illuminating your path.

Shamans, witches, and some spiritual practitioners use fire to perform magic and rituals. While some used fire to bring peace and become more creative, others used it for purposes like casting spells. Typically, fire is used for noble needs in the spiritual realm. Shamans and witches realized and decoded the beauty and fiery nature of fire and used it for their betterment. It takes a lot of time, practice, and determination to harness the magic of fire and manipulate it to reap maximum benefits. To perform fire magic, all practitioners use some form of tools, such as axes, incense, swords, or sticks.

Fire thrives without any specific intention—it can either create or destroy depending on the way it is handled. If used in the right way, it can illuminate your path. On the flipside, mishandling it can destroy or burn everything down. Fire does not have any remorse and attracts people toward its blazing and gorgeous reddish-yellow hues. According to Greek philosophy, fire is one of the four most important elements necessary for existence. It thrives in harmony with Earth, Air, and Water, all of which are important too. Our soul is constantly searching for fire and purity, which is defined as "enlightenment" according to Greek philosophy.

Several mythologies and cultures point out the correlation between fire and living creatures. In cultural stories, many gods, giants, creatures, and beasts are related to the power of fire or its qualities. For example, Roman deities like Vulcan and Vesta, Greek deities like Hestia and Hephaestus, and Celtic deities like Brighid and Bel were related to fire. Several accounts also mention dragons, phoenixes, and other mythic beasts that emit fire or were related to the element. Norse mythology, in particular, stressed the creation and destruction process of the universe and attributed it to fire and ice. These elements are essential for the creation and resurrection of the cosmos. Some Norse myths also tell the story of fire giants, deities, and relevant energies.

In this book, you will learn about fire as an element and its magical properties. Every chapter covers information about different topics related to fire. We will begin by talking about fire magic and its significance, followed by its symbolization and characteristics. In the next chapter, you will learn about several different fire entities, including deities, beasts, dragons, and elementals. As you will proceed, you will gain insights into setting up a fire altar with great precision and taking the correct precautions.

You will also learn about fire herbs, plants, crystals, and gemstones and the right way to use them to harness the power of fire. The next chapters will walk you through the fire element as perceived and used in Norse mythology and Pagan festivals. Lastly, you will also learn to use some spells and perform your own fire rituals to get positive results.

If you are intrigued and want to know more about the significance of the fire element through magic, turn the pages and get started.

Chapter 1: What Is Fire Magic?

Depending on the way you handle the element, fire can either be destructive or creative. Despite being intrinsically dangerous, its beauty and mysterious nature ignite one's curiosity. If handled carefully, fire can bring light and help you to carve your path. It also gives you warmth on a dark, cold day. However, if mishandled, a tiny flame can burn everything and bring it down. This is why fire should be respected.

Among all four elements (earth, fire, air, and water), fire is the most dangerous and can be an unstable element to deal with. Manipulating fire can be extremely difficult, especially if it is used for noble purposes. However, the practitioner must be very careful when conjuring using fire for witchcraft.

The History of Fire Magic

Pagans and practitioners have been using fire to perform rituals for centuries. From reading minds to summoning the dead, the element has been manipulated for various reasons. In fact, the art of fire magic has evolved significantly over the centuries, so much so that the craft was an integral part of several civilizations. The magical properties of the fire element vary according to the needs, usage, practice, and tradition. It also evokes different sentiments for practitioners. Some consider the fire element as a person's success, whereas others relate internal cleansing and emotions with fire flames. Rituals relating to fire were also performed by practitioners at the Temple of Athena.

In Greek mythology, Prometheus entered heaven to steal fire and spread its energy to humankind, thereby promoting life on earth. This is also why fire is associated with power, energy, passion, and willpower. Over time, fire was perceived as an essential resource, as it promoted fertility, life, warmth, and comfort. In the Middle Ages, the element was linked to the solar disk and summer days.

Fire Deities

Every culture worshipped its own fire deity who represented passion, heat, inspiration, and desire. The vibrational nature of fire and flames inspired worshippers and helped them carve their path through life. Some of the most prominent fire deities included Chango, Agni, Di Penates, Kali, Bast, Astarte, Pele, and Vulcan. Our ancestors were inspired by the Sun's energy and heat to ignite tribal fires and create rituals. Over time, shamanic witches and practitioners used the power of fire to enter the spiritual realm. The vibrational energy of fire was believed to heal or destroy other energies. Practitioners developed tricks and magic rituals to harness the element's power.

Superstitions

In the past, people formed a lot of superstitions in association with the fire element. Midsummer, Beltane, and other ancient festivals often focused on fire and related superstitions. Baal Fires were ignited in some Celtic regions to keep their animal herds healthy and safe. People encouraged their herd to move between the Baal Fires as they believed that the element's power would keep them healthy. Today, it is believed that seeing fire and flames in your dreams can have several connotations. For instance, if you see yourself walking through fire without any harm or burns, you may have the strength to deal with tumultuous times.

Fire and Other Elements

According to Western magical traditions and Wicca, fire is associated with three other elements: air, water, and earth. The fifth element is spirit and forms a symbiotic relationship with fire. Greek cosmology and philosophy stressed the importance of just four elements that made up the universe, which were fire, earth, air, and water. The human body also represents these four elements in different proportions. The microcosm arrangement pattern is intricately connected to the macrocosm level of the universe and nature. The element of earth thrives in a solid state, air in a gaseous state, fire in an igneous state, and water in a liquid state.

Fire and Earth

The Earth is our home, where all living beings thrive and find food and other resources for their survival. Earth's density and heaviness gravitates other sources toward its surface. Collectively, fire and earth make objects more discrete by separating them. Fire distills, refines, and transforms objects, whereas earth coagulates, condenses, and solidifies. The hot and cold nature of fire and earth, respectively, can be challenging yet essential to survival.

Fire and Air

When the universe was a void, Æther filled the spaces, and the air was supposed to be linked with this component. Since all other components were absent in the beginning, air was believed to exist first. Since Æther and air were often interchangeable, Empedocles proved that air is a separate entity by showing an experiment of an inverted water bowl to create air pockets. Some philosophers denoted Æther to be the fifth element. Air exists above the earth and water spheres, where people move and live.

The association of fire and air is symbiotic. Without air, one cannot light a fire. The resultant quality can be called "hot" as the association produces a lot of heat and warmth. In essence, air represents movement, contact, and exchange. No one can survive without air, which is why it is an essential component of life. Collectively, fire and air are energetic, subtle, and light. They move in harmony and sway together. Fire primarily depends on air to become more powerful.

Fire and Water

Just like earth, water is dense and heavy too. Water runs on and under the Earth's surface and can be accessed from rivers, lakes, and oceans. It keeps the Earth moist and provides nourishment for food to grow. It is also an essential element for survival. Unlike air and fire, which are "hot" in nature, water and earth are "cold" and substantial. Fire and water are completely opposite in nature and act as Yin and Yang—two opposite forces that thrive in harmony. The hot and fiery nature of fire can be destroyed by the wet and cold nature of water. If the fire is too destructive, we use water to calm the force. Collectively, both elements represent change and manifestation. They govern major physical and metabolic processes, which are important for survival.

Æther: The Fifth Element

As mentioned, Greek philosophy identifies Æther as the fifth element associated with space. It is the most refined and lightest element of all. It is the womb, primary source, or "Prima Materia" responsible for creating the universe. It is believed to exist since the beginning and is responsible for manifestation. Being dry and cold, Æther predominantly shares attributes with earth and partly with water. However, it is subtle and light, just like fire.

The Role of Fire Magic and Rituals

In the world of magic, spells, and paganism, the element is held in high esteem and used in creative ways to achieve desired results. Hearth fires, lanterns, torches, bonfires, sparklers, and candle flames are some tools used to perform fire spells. As mentioned, handling fire is not an easy task. The way it sways and changes shape can impact and trigger the practitioner's emotions, which can affect the end results. The element can evoke multiple emotions all at once, like desire, passion, anger, or motivation.

In essence, Fire magic was performed to fulfill the following positive goals:

- Enhancing personal energy or rebuilding it.
- Improving personal relationships.
- Seeking happiness and compassion.
- Finding the truth (specifically inner or spiritual truth).
- Finding inspiration or motivation.
- Blocking negative energy, vibrations, and thoughts.
- Enhancing self-image and seeking self-improvement.
- Protecting yourself and your close ones.
- Boosting self-confidence and self-awareness.
- Building power and strength to win.
- Removing the negative effect of curses.

Even though Fire magic was predominantly used to fulfill positive goals, some people performed it for evil purposes, like:

- Taking revenge.
- Casting curses.
- Banishing enemies.
- Evoking a destructive force.
- Developing intimidation.

The Ancient Art of Pyromancy

This art is used to summon the dead, primarily to know more about the deceased one's past and get in touch with their spirit remains. Pyromancy is associated with "fire divinity" and was implemented for both noble and evil purposes. Among several types and variations of this witchcraft, the most basic include the interpretation of silhouettes and shapes in candle flames. The art of casting salt into flames when performing Pyromancy is called alomancy. Along with salt, practitioners also add other components to fire, some of which include laurel leaves (or other plant parts), straw, and turtle shells.

The Conjuring of Fire

Since flames sway uncontrollably and constantly, especially in windy weather conditions, they need to be controlled for provenance. Typically, shamans and witches use two wooden sticks to control the flames. The ritual includes tapping the two sticks and chanting a mantra or rhyme. This brings the fire in their complete control, after which they can conjure the element to fulfill their desires.

Hearth Magic and Fire Scrying

Individuals represented by the fire sign in their horoscope can use the heat from the Sun to cook, bake, and brew items. Hearth witchcraft combines mundane kitchen activities with the power of nature to make one's living space more sacred and peaceful. Some Hearth witches are also constantly involved in candle-making, weaving, and cooking with fire. Fire scrying is the art of staring in the fire to achieve divination. Typically, practitioners use a small candle with a stable flame to perform this ritual. Mastering the art of fire scrying can take a few months to years.

Other practices like metal alchemy, incense, and smudging were also popular rituals among practitioners and witches.

Characteristics and Symbolization of Fire

Fire symbolizes manifestation, action, and the physical body and its related attributes. In a spiritual sense, the element represents creativity, compulsion, passion, and zeal. If used properly, fire can awaken and engage all your senses, increasing your drive to accomplish goals and stay motivated. Fire is linked to specific colors, star signs, metals, directions, planets, and tools, which can help strengthen your knowledge and ability to perform magic.

Colors

The element corresponds with shades of heat, which are red, a variety of oranges, and yellow. Some fires portray deep yellow hues, whereas others display sparks of dark red and orange. Once you learn to decode the element's shades, you can easily interpret its action and nature. A yellow fire can be associated with the higher power or the soul of divinity. Deep red flames and sparks over a fire can mean aggressiveness, courage, or burning desire. If the fire is predominantly orange in color, you may find inspiration through incentive or action. To understand more about the colors, read up about the different hues and learn to interpret your fire's shades to understand your inner self. Collectively, the hues blend to make a golden color, which is why molten gold is also linked to the fire element.

Since the air element ignites and the fire element feeds on it, colors like blue and white are also mildly associated with fire. These contrasting colors blend to represent the mixed and exuberant nature of fire. The red and yellow hues on the top sway in excitement and passion, whereas the blue and white hues uplift the flames and push them toward glory. This can, however, confuse beginners who are stepping into the magical world of fire rituals. They must understand the blend of hues and visible colors to decipher the complex nature of the fire element.

Planets and Zodiac Signs

Fire is predominantly associated with the planets Mars, Jupiter, and the Sun. Jupiter and Mars are also intricately connected to water signs and are co-ruled by both elements. The Sun represents our central qualities and drives our primary path. Jupiter inspires us to learn more and expand our knowledge. Mars keeps our aggression and desires uplifted, which is exactly what the fire element represents. The three zodiac signs related to the fire sign are Leo, Aries, and Sagittarius. If you are born under any of these zodiac signs and represented by the fire sign, you are likely dynamic and passionate by nature. People with these star signs tend to possess an immense capacity to love but can get extremely angry as well.

Direction

According to Vedic astrology and Vastu Shastra, the fire element (Agni) represents the southern direction. The Sun is deemed to be "the giver of life," which is also why it is responsible for a person's vitality and strength. As you know, the Sun and the fire element are intricately connected as well. According to Vastu, fire can make or break a person's home, office, and shop, which is why you must use it carefully. Vastu experts suggest building your kitchen in the southeast direction as it represents "Agneya." Some even suggest painting the wall in the south direction with a dark red shade due to the color's connotation with fire.

Metals

Brass, gold, and steel are the three main metals represented by fire. In essence, fire is related to sulfur, one of the chemical elements in alchemy. This is why fire's alchemical symbol is an upward-pointing triangle. According to alchemic logic and tradition, the Earth's womb makes and incubates all metals mined from the ground. The fire in the womb protects the metals and helps them mature for a long period. Alchemists use these metals to expand their growth and indulge in deep introspection to find their inner qualities. Gold, in particular, is also associated with the Sun and was an important metal since ancient Egyptian times.

Crystals

The fire element represents Gold, Fire Opal, Ruby, Bloodstone, Tiger's Eye, Carnelian, Amber, Garnet, and Sunstone. Some lesser-known gemstones and crystals associated with fire are Agate, Sulfur, Quartz, Thunderstone, Rhodochrosite, Red Jasper, Obsidian, and Star Garnet. If you want to harness the magical and positive powers of fire, wear one of these crystals as a pendant, a ring, or any other piece of jewelry. You can also keep it by your bedside and cleanse it regularly to harness its maximum potential. Depending on the type of outcome desired by practitioners, they often wear a similar gemstone or crystal when performing rituals.

Tools

Witches and shamans perform fire rituals and spells using wands or incense sticks, which are also the two main types of tools for fire magic. However, fire is closely related to swords, athame, daggers, and candles. Some witches prefer to use tools extremely specific to certain rituals. These include lanterns, matches, lightning bolt imagery, axes, burn safe containers, alcohol, ash, black salt, fairy lights, electrical appliances, leather, whips, sun imagery, a fire pit, knives, a lava lamp, spatulas, skillets, wax melters, tea lights, volcano imagery, and a wooden spoon. Some of these tools are commonly used in several practices, especially in pyromancy.

Plants

Some plants related to the fire element are rue, thistle, basil, cactus, rosemary, coffee beans, and peppers. Some lesser-known plants and herbs associated with fire are peppermint, cinnamon, nettles, onion, hibiscus, garlic, red poppy, clove, almond, sunflower, chamomile, oak, holly, and bay leaf. Some of these herbs and plants need a lot of heat to grow, thereby validating their association with fire. Witches use some of these spices and herbs to perform fire magic and achieve a favorable outcome. Most strong-smelling or fiery spices are used with stronger spells and rituals as they possess the ability to protect from or banish curses.

Animals

Crickets, bees, scorpions, lizards, and snakes remind one of fire. Other animals loosely associated with fire are lions, tigers, dragons, and ladybugs. The mythical animal, the phoenix, is believed to have risen from the ashes and is illustrated with fire on its wings. Some of these animals are actually made of fire, whereas others are associated with the element in terms of seasons, qualities, or living conditions. Other mythological creatures connected with fire are the chimera (a fire-breathing creature of Lycia) and griffin. In most cultures, the association between animals and fire comes from a comparison of physical traits instead of inner qualities.

Body Parts

Our metabolic system and loins are connected to fire. Other body parts related to fire are the stomach, arms, muscles, blood, heart, head, and eyes. The element of fire engages your taste and sight. Among all body parts, fire specifically rules the heart as it is known to be the center of warmth, comfort, and kindness. A person feels using their heart, which is probably why people failing to portray emotions are often called "cold-hearted" or "heartless." Just like fire, the heart can either be happy, selfless, and kind, or selfish, hateful, and cruel. The outcome and qualities depend on the way it is handled.

Numerology: Fire and the Number 11

The number of insights, illumination, and vibrations—the numeral 11 is linked to the fire element. Just like fire represents deep passion and illumination, the number 11 reveals the spiritual truth too. Furthermore, 11 can either create or destroy a person's future, just like fire. Those who are associated with number 11 in numerology are blessed with great physical and mental aptitude. The number 11 is well-respected in ancient and modern numerology. Just like fire, the number should be kept on a stable keel to achieve a sense of protection and warmth. By contrast, an unattended number can burn out or cause harm.

Tarot

The Suit of Wands in Tarot cards is linked to fire, if you draw one of these cards during your reading it means that you are passionate or undergoing alchemical transformation. The Tower and Devil Tarot Cards in the Major Arcana illustrate fire as their main symbol. It can mean that you may soon be given responsibilities or bear great power. Your ambition, insights, strengths, and growth are represented by these Tarot cards, all of which are also characterized by the fire element. The wand can point inward or outward, representing our inner desires and shining light like a fire. It also inspires us to take up our incomplete tasks and finish them at the earliest possible time.

All in all, the element of fire is associated with warmth, joy, brightness, youth, red, vocalization, growth, expansion, integration, motivation, meditation, and the direction south. Fire is neither "noble" nor "evil"; it is just the way it is. However, the way you manipulate and apply fire to rituals and magic can significantly change its nature. Fire stands and shines in its own glory. It demands respect and proper care. If you use it in the right way, it can empower your soul, give it warmth, and help you to live a bright or enlightened life.

Chapter 2: Fire Entities – Dragons, Deities, and Elementals

In many cultures, fire is closely associated with different entities, from deities to mythical beasts to real-life animals. The tales of these mythological creatures have been passed down through the centuries. Because they are supposed to possess tremendous powers, the stories of their existence often serve various purposes. Building communities, safeguarding treasures, or passing these stories onto children to continue cultural beliefs are only a few reasons behind the creation of these mythological creatures. This chapter will cover different entities that have played a significant role in fire magic. Some of these creatures originate from fire, while others are able to produce fire or extend their abilities through it in other ways.

Mythical Creatures

Salamanders

Unlike many other fire creatures, a salamander is both a mythical beast and a real animal. It's also elemental, an entity connected to one of nature's main elements through magical means. Like most amphibians, salamanders hibernate during winter, and they often do this in hollow logs that people collect for fuel. When tossed onto the flames, a salamander will wake up and run away from the fire, making it look like it's born from it.

Muséum de Toulouse, CC BY-SA 4.0 <https://creativecommons.org/licenses/by-sa/4.0>, via Wikimedia Commons
https://commons.wikimedia.org/wiki/File:Salamandra_salamandra_MHNT_1.jpg

Salamander

According to some myths, a salamander has magical skin that protects it from a fire. Other tales might say that the animal's incredible ability to lower its body temperature allows it not only to escape from a fire but to extinguish it as well, and not only can they manipulate fire, but they are also able to send messages through it. In some ancient cultures, incense from herbs was used to communicate with salamanders, who then carried the messages to the spiritual world. This ritual was often used to connect with an ancestral spirit and keep the connection warm through emotions.

Phoenix

The phoenix is one of the most commonly known creatures associated with fire in the mythology of many different civilizations. Most depictions of the phoenix are that of a bird with plumage in vivid orange, with scarlet to darker red tail feathers. While there are legends from all over the world mentioning an ancient bird that closely resembled the phoenix, there is no tangible evidence that such an animal ever existed in real life.

Nearing the end of its life, the phoenix is said to collect twigs for a nest which essentially becomes the bird's funeral pyre. Suddenly, the phoenix catches on fire, and its body perishes in flames. From the ashes that remain after the death of the bird, a new phoenix is born, and its life cycle is continued.

According to myths, the phoenix is a creature possessing infinite wisdom, which has been accumulated during its unusually long lifespan. Practitioners of fire magic often rely on the phoenix's knowledge and consult this sacred bird for answers to pressing questions in their life.

Firebird

Despite popular belief, the phoenix isn't the only bird that has been associated with fire in mythology. Similar to the phoenix, the firebird is also depicted with warm-colored feathers. However, the symbolization of the feathers is entirely different in the case of a firebird. It's said that its feathers can emanate an incredible amount of light. In fact, one single feather is enough to light up a dark room, regardless of its size.

Some tales say that the firebird's ability to light things up can also be applied to other aspects of life. For example, the bird's fire magic can be used to rejuvenate lands and reveal a hidden treasure. Other myths claim that the firebird can bring doom to its captor. But, let free, it will shower its saviors with blessings. Because of this, the firebird has been coveted by many, including warriors who have been on an endless number of quests to obtain either the bird itself or at least its magical feathers.

The Chimera

The Chimera is described in Greek Mythology as a three-headed creature, with each head resembling a distorted version of a real animal. According to myths, this trait was passed down to the Chimera from its father, Typhon, a half-beast, half-human with a thousand heads. From its mother, Echidna, the creature inherited a gruesome, serpentine-like tail that moved with lightning speed.

The Chimera is said to live near volcanoes—and like dragons, it breathes out terrible fires, which could reach amazingly high temperatures. However, this creature was rarely able to control the flames, nor was it inclined to communicate with humans. Many tales describe the chimera wreaking havoc due to minor provocations. Not only could the creature melt everything around it when it opened all of its three heads, but its tail was able to demolish entire mountains. People living near mountains would always do everything they could to avoid provoking the Chimera.

The Kapre

While most mythological creatures related to fire are described as having animal characteristics, the Kapre is said to have humanoid features. Although close to nine feet tall, according to Philippine mythology, this entity still resembles a human. So much so that it's said that it often confuses tourists who stop and ask it for directions. A Kapre can distract a traveler by sending them the wrong direction and by lighting little magical fires that can be mistaken for streetlights.

The Kapre is also said to lure in women by smoking a pipe filled with sweet-smelling perfume and lit with magical fire. Since it is said to inhabit forests, the unique smell is quite distinctive in the environment—and can be very alluring to unsuspecting women. The Kapre uses a belt that provides it with the power of invisibility. Due to this, it will gain the ability to blend in with the trees, so its victim won't be able to spot it until it's too late.

Fire Giants

Fire giants are usually depicted as enormous human-like creatures that live in the mountains in warmer climates. They were also often thought to have claws and fangs, which made them quite scary-looking. While sometimes ferocious in nature, perhaps because of their close connection to a warm element, fire giants are said to be benevolent and full of wisdom. The latter may also be the result of their lifespan of more than 300 years and their ability to socialize while living in small groups.

According to most illustrations, their bright orange hair resembles a glowing flame and has magical abilities. Apart from this, it was also possible for these creatures to use their inner magical fire on other objects. When they were attacked by an enemy, the fire giants defended themselves by letting their body heat seep into the rocks nearby. When these rocks caught on fire, they obliterated any threat to the giants.

The Cherufe

Tales of a gigantic monster connected with fire originating from Chilean mythology portray a creature living in the base of volcanoes. The name of this entity is Cherufe, and it is said to be shaped like a man-made hot magma. Its origins could probably be explained by the ancient Chileans' need to have an explanation for natural phenomena like earthquakes and volcanoes. They looked for signs in the supernatural world, and the Cherufe was born.

People living near the volcanoes believed that earthquakes and volcanic eruptions were the result of Cherufe being angry. Not only was this creature feared because it could destroy entire villages that were in the path of melting lava, but it was also thought to have an appetite for young women. So, to stop the creature from causing more earthquakes and volcanic eruptions, it would have to be fed. And the Cherufe could only be satisfied with sacrifices involving throwing young women into the mouth of the volcano.

Fire Serpent

Similar to many other cultures, Aztec mythology also contains stories depicting mythological beasts connected with fire. Although it is only one of the many serpents associated with fire, Xiuhcoatl, the fire serpent, is one of the most prevalent fire entities. It's usually described as having an elongated, segmented body ending in a somewhat distorted muzzle. The shape of its snout made it possible for the creature to emit flames out of its fanged mouth.

British Museum, CC BY 2.0 <https://creativecommons.org/licenses/by/2.0>, via Wikimedia Commons
https://commons.wikimedia.org/wiki/File:Double_Headed_Serpent_Aztec_BM.jpg

Fire Serpent

The Xiulcoatl has many possible origins—and because there is a lack of historical evidence in general about Aztec traditions, it's hard to give more credit to any in particular. In one myth, the Xiuhcoatl represented a spiritual form of Xiuhtecuhtli, the Aztec God governing fire. According to other tales, the fire serpent is associated with the Mexican God of Fire and the Sun. Yet another story depicts it as a two-headed creature—with one head representing Earth and the other one natural catastrophes.

Celtic Deities

Bel

Known as the God of Fire, Sun, and healing, Bel was the most widely worshipped of all Celtic Gods. According to Celtic lore, he was able to move the Sun across the sky to bring out its warmth. This provided enough sunlight for the crops to grow and for the people to be fed. However, Bel was also able to create fire, and if he was provoked, he would throw lightning bolts across the sky. To ensure a good harvest and prevent their crops from burning, sacrifices were often offered to Bel. In Celtic culture, it was equally important to express gratitude after a plentiful harvest, as it was to pray for good weather during the warmer months.

Not only was he able to make the Sun appear, but Bel was also praised for his abilities to create healing fires. Celtic witches and healers drew strength from Bel when using healing magic. When doing this, the most effective way to use his power was to seek it out during a ritual that has its origin in the use of fire. A person suffering from an illness or injury would recover much more quickly after being warmed by sunlight and receiving a cure made over a flame blessed by Bel. To this day, Bel is said to be able to cure physical ailments and purify one's soul as well.

Brigid

Brigid was the Celtic Goddess of fire, representing the sacred nature of hearth fire, which is said to provide emotional warmth to any home. She was also a patron of poets and healers, and witches using fire magic. In fact, many contemporary witches still use Brigid's power for prophecy and divination. These practitioners believe that as long as there's someone to keep Brigid alive in their hearts, the Goddess will bless them with power.

https://pixabay.com/sv/photos/l%C3%A5gor-brand-kvinna-inflammerad-2765680/

Brigid

In Ireland, Brigid was honored with a sacred flame near a sacred oak tree surrounded by a dense hedge. The fire was tended for centuries by nineteen priestesses serving Brigid, who took turns, each of them feeding the fire on a different day. Once, the fire was mistakenly left alone on the twentieth day, but it never went out, proving to all followers that Brigid was watching over it at all times.

When the first fire was extinguished against the followers' will, many other flames dedicated to Brigid were lit in holy wells across the country. Some of these wells are still standing and are considered pure and sacred places where followers can pay homage to Brigid by throwing small objects into them as offerings. It's also believed that heating water from any of these wells over a flame blessed by Brigid has magical healing abilities.

Greek Deities

Hephaestus

Hephaestus was the Greek God of fire, and he would usually manifest himself as a natural power of a physical nature. Whether it was governing over volcanic territories or controlling a fire used in arts and creativity, his blessing became indispensable for the Greeks. Being a delicate creature from birth, Hephaestus overcame many difficulties and became capable of many things—much like when a fire arises from a tiny spark. Once a fire was blessed by him, it was called the breath of Hephaestus and was able to provide a means for creating the most beautiful things in life.

It's also believed that Hephaestus taught mortals many arts and gave them skills that they could use to make a living and improve someone's life. Artists all around ancient Greece prayed to him for a blessing to be able to create objects that everyone could appreciate. Offerings were often made to Hephaestus, including celebratory meals.

Hephaestus was said to have a tremendous influence on fires occurring in nature, such as volcanic eruptions. Therefore, he had to be kept satisfied at all times with praise and sacrifices. After all, due to the unpredictable nature of volcanoes, people never knew when they may need his help to divert the fire from their homes.

Hestia

Often referred to as the virgin Goddess, Hestia personified the fire burning in the hearths of homes in ancient Greece. Despite being one of the twelve powerful deities of Greek mythology, Hestia inspired nothing more than for followers to tend to her divine home. Being so focused on domestic life, she became the representation of all the security and happiness a hearth provided for individuals and communities alike.

Her name means "hearth" since she governed fire while focusing on families and communities. As an homage to this, the fire around which people have often gathered became known as the hearth and a unique representation of their bond. Families and communities often made Hestia the first offering at every sacrificial ritual by leaving the richest portion of food and their sweetest wine for her. Even meals without sacrifice have often begun with praise of gratitude for Hestia.

Once a fire was blessed by Hestia, it was considered magical, and it was not allowed to go out, unless extinguishing it was part of an intentional ritual. If the flame died, the magic keeping the family or the community together was lost, and the people would lose their sense of belonging. For this reason, not only were the hearths in family homes fed constantly, but the public hearth dedicated to Hestia was to be kept alive at all times.

Roman Deities

Vesta

Vesta is the Roman Goddess of fire, who—similar to her Greek counterpart—was also identified with the domestic tranquility a fire can provide to a home. For the ancient Romans, the hearth fire in their household was much more than a means for cooking food and heating. Apart from being the place for eating, the kitchen also served as the gathering place for the family and friends. Consequently, its hearth was meant to provide comfort and intimacy. Often, families prayed here to their ancestral spirits—which was only possible with the blessing from Vesta. If a fire burned in a hearth was enriched with magic, the meals were fulfilling, and the family could bond together even more effectively.

https://pixabay.com/vectors/vesta-ancient-greek-mythology-146933/

Vesta

To make sure they could earn Vesta's blessings, the Romans made sacrifices to her and threw these into the flames. Some followers made objects with the help of the fire and presented these as offerings to the Goddess. If someone from the family left their home for a longer period of time, they carried some of the blessed hearth fire with them to keep their home and family close at all times. Since the task of carrying around a live flame proved to be quite challenging, travelers often stopped and prayed for Vesta to help them keep their home fires burning.

Vulcan

Vulcan was known as the deformed Roman God governing fire and one of the highest members of the council of Gods. He rose to this position due to creating all magical weapons and objects of beauty while he worked as the blacksmith of the Gods. According to myths,

Vulcan had the ability to control the fire and was able to shape and direct it in any way. Not only was he able to bless the work of blacksmiths and artists working with fire, but he had an influence on fires occurring in nature.

The Romans erected several shrines in honor of Vulcan and used them to make sacrifices to Vulcan so he would shield their crops from fire. Blacksmiths and artists have prayed to him often as well. If Vulcan blessed their fire with magic, they were able to produce pieces and earn their living from them. Since these rituals often involved celebratory fires, these shrines were located outside of the city. This way, if Vulcan's fiery temper was provoked, he couldn't direct the fire into the city.

Vulcanalia was an ancient Roman festival that also stemmed from the need to placate Vulcan. When a volcanic eruption caused a great fire in Rome, the belief was that the God of fire was responsible, and the resulting eruptions of a volcano grew even larger.

The Role of Dragons in Fire Magic

Despite there not being any proof that such creatures ever existed, dragons probably played one of the most significant roles in fire mythology. While some cultures see these large, scaly-bodied creatures as evil beings, others add positive spiritual qualities to them. Most depictions agree, however, that dragons are quite intelligent and can understand human nature. This made it possible for humans to communicate with them, ask them for favors and, according to some tales, even use them in battles.

Apart from tremendous strength and the ability to breathe fire, dragons were often associated with other supernatural abilities as well. Some were able to predict the future, while others had an elemental connection. The dragons connected to nature are often described by the color of the element they govern. Red dragons were most commonly associated with fire and were said to have immense control over it. Not only were they able to breathe fire of different temperatures, but they could also control the shape of this unpredictable element. Said to live near volcanoes in hot climates, red dragons were often seen as protectors of human civilizations.

However, due to their fiery temperament, dragons also have a somewhat unpredictable nature, which means that if provoked, they can also destroy anything around them. In many cultures, offerings were made to placate the dragons governing fire, so they wouldn't turn against the people. Some tales even describe the magical fire the red dragon produces and controls as being sacred. According to these stories, praising dragons could not only prevent misuse of fire but other elemental disturbances as well.

Chapter 3: Setting Up a Fire Altar Safely

We've all seen rituals that involve candles, but how many people think of setting up an altar specifically to burn candles or incense? Setting up an altar specifically for fire magic may seem like overkill, but it can be a powerful addition to your arsenal of ritual tools when done correctly.

Building a Fire Alter

Depending on what you want to use your fire altar for, when you build it, it must be in the shape of a box and have ornate carvings or paintings on the outside to display your dedication to that sort of fire magic. Inside it can hold candles, incense burners, braziers, cauldrons for burning offerings, and whatever you find necessary for ritual work.

It's important to keep in mind that this is a fire altar, and you should treat it with respect, which such a thing demands. That means not allowing pets and children near it. Also, do not rest anything flammable on top of your altar.

What Can the Fire Alter Be Used For?

If you want to set up an altar for ritual work but not magic itself, consider keeping your fire offerings simple. One candle in one holder is more than enough and can be used to help mark time during rituals that may run over schedule. Use a holder that is stable, with a flat surface underneath.

It is important to note that if you keep a candle on the top of your altar, especially if you light it and leave it unattended—which is not recommended—there is always the chance that someone will bump into it or knock it over. Make sure nothing flammable is around that could pose a risk.

Fire Offerings and Their Uses

This depends largely on the sort of magic you are doing. If you're doing anything that involves petitioning or speaking to a deity, try to get into a dialogue or pray to the deity after lighting your offering in the form of a candle. Let them know exactly what it is you want and why, and be sure to give them time to respond.

If you're not petitioning a deity, use your fire offerings as you see fit. If you want to purify an area, light a candle, and leave it to burn for a little while. If you're looking to cleanse yourself of bad luck or negative energies, try burning some incense. Always remember that the best way to petition a deity is through cultural understanding and tradition, so try to have a set of guidelines on how you should use fire magic.

Incense Burners

If you've ever been in a spiritual or religious setting, the odds are good that you've seen an incense burner being used at least once. Use them as necessary during your rituals, but be careful not to overdo them. Burning too much incense can make your space smell strongly, which isn't very conducive to any kind of magic. If you do use an incense burner during the ritual, try placing it on the floor or on some other sturdy surface that is fireproof and where it is not easily knocked over. Also, keep in mind that incense burners make terrible candle holders. Please do not set anything else on top of them, especially candles.

What about Large Cauldrons?

Cauldrons are awesome for rituals, but you must treat them with the proper respect. Never get your altar or any fire tools you may have placed on it wet. If you're working with water in your cauldron, be sure to put it into the cauldron only after a candle has been lit and is starting to burn down. What this does is provide you with an oil lamp effect. The fire keeps the water boiling without ever spilling over or getting out of control.

If you want to use your cauldron to store offerings or any other sort of liquid, try using an old rag as a plug. If you'd rather not use a rag, find something else you can use, such as a rock (just make sure it's clean), and keep an eye on your cauldron for the next few days. If you notice any drips coming down from where you put the plug in, remove it immediately and clean out your cauldron. Without proper precautions, fire offerings can cause a lot of damage, so take care.

The Importance of an Altar

An altar is a simple thing. All it takes to make an altar is something flat and fireproof on which you can keep your tools and offerings. You don't need anything fancy or extraordinary. Just remember that if you have kids or pets, be sure to place the altar high and out of their reach. It's also important to note that in most religions and cultures, altars are placed facing south. This is because, in the northern hemisphere, the sun spends more time in the southern part of the sky than in any other direction.

Many people will tell you to clear an area before beginning a ritual because it removes outside distractions. While this is certainly sound advice, consider how much room you will need for yourself. If you're planning on doing a ritual by yourself, be sure to remove anything that might distract you during the process and leave an open space in which to move around and do your magic safely.

Altars help you to center yourself and get you into the right frame of mind for your ritual. If you're just trying to clear away clutter or do some sort of meditation, that's great. But if you're trying to cast a spell and bring about actual change in your life, it's important to make sure your altar is properly set up beforehand.

Tools and How to Use Them

First and foremost, an altar is not a place for sharp items like pins or needles, no matter how magically inclined you may be. This includes things like knives, swords, and staffs that have been sharpened to a point, or anything else that may cut or pierce someone during a ritual.

Remember your altar should be kept as clean as possible. Remove any leftover incense from previous rituals, candles that have burned down, and anything else you may have used for other purposes. Anything you use regularly should be cleaned before it is replaced on the altar, if your items can be washed or wiped down without harming them.

One way to symbolize fire on your tools is with the image of a lightning bolt.

The Tools Used for Fire and Their Importance

Bagua Mirror: This is a simple thing to use and can be found just about anywhere that sells Feng Shui items. Simply place it on your altar to face south, and you'll find that your magic will start to focus more on everything it represents. You can also use it to see things, either in the past or in the future.

Buddha: The Buddha represents all kinds of things, including water and earth. That said, it's best not to place one that's made of jade or other semi-precious stones on your altar due to its water element. If you do so, the lightning symbol on its chest should always face south, thus protecting your altar from any forces that may damage it.

Candles: While they are not required for a ritual, candles can be used in just about any magic work you wish to accomplish. They represent air by way of fire, and their flame is the element that we call upon in most of our spells and rituals. Make sure you place them where they can't be knocked over easily and don't burn anything other than the candle itself.

Cauldron: This represents water, and when placed on your altar, make sure it faces north so that the lightning bolt pendant on its handle faces south. This ensures that all the water spirits will hear your call and come to do your bidding.

Censer: Fire and air are always found in this much-needed tool to complete a spell or ritual. It's best to make sure it isn't made of metal, however, due to its connection to the earth and its ability to harm you. Stone censers are the best choice for this reason, but if none are available, you can use wooden ones instead.

Cup: This represents water by way of its liquid contents, which is why it should be filled with nothing less than pure water at any given time. Like cauldrons and other tools that hold liquids, this should face north so that the lightning bolt on its handle faces south.

Sword: The sword represents fire in all of its forms, which is why it must be placed with the blade facing east. That way, any flames you use to complete a spell will always be pointed in the correct direction for full effect when you've finished your ritual.

Staff: The staff represents earth, which is why it should always face west when placed on your altar. This allows the lightning bolt on its top to face east and thus be ready for anything you may need to call upon the element of air for, including spells that require wind or storms.

Mirror: Although there are many different kinds of mirrors, all of them can be used effectively when placed on your altar so that the spell you want to cast is reflected onto your target. In this way, they represent air by way of water, and their lightning bolt should always face south for reasons similar to those involving cauldrons.

Hexagram: Place this in a prominent place on your altar so that it acts as a guardian (not only to the south but also to your altar). You can use this for protection or to call upon spirits of fire, particularly the spirit kings who are always good for favors in magic work.

Pyramid: This should be placed on your altar facing east and acts as a portal to other dimensions when used with fire magic. It's best to use this sparingly, however, as it can take you to places you don't want to be or that you may not return from for some time.

Temple: This is the centerpiece of your altar and should be placed with some distance between it and all other objects in your workspace. It represents fire as well as water, which is why a stone construction should be used in most situations.

Tower: When you need to burn something down or wish to tear open the veil between worlds for a short amount of time, this is an ideal object on your altar. Just make sure that its lightning bolt faces south when you're finished using it so that nothing unexpected happens in the process.

Triangle: This is a universal symbol that can be used in many different circumstances. It represents fire and air, much like the wand, but has more applications than any other device on your altar. For this reason, you should always keep it within arm's reach when working with fire magic.

Water: This element is best represented by clear water in a crystal vase that's been decorated with a lightning bolt. This allows for a window between worlds to be created, which can lead to better communication with spirits or more power in your magic when dealing with fire.

In addition to these tools, you'll also need wax, incense, and oil on hand at all times to complete any spell you want to cast. Though it's not technically part of the altar, you should always keep paper and a writing instrument nearby to record your spells and then burn them once the spell is complete so that nobody else can use them in an undesirable manner.

Before you begin any fire magic work on your altar, take some time to think about what you're trying to accomplish and ask yourself the following questions:

- Am I casting this spell safely?

- Is fire magic the best way to solve my problem or get what I want?

- Am I confident that no allergies will be triggered by something used in this spell, such as pollen from flowers or cedar from incense?

- Am I prepared to deal with any consequences that may happen as a result of working fire magic, including ghosts or spirits who may be attracted to me?

If you can answer no to any of those questions, then it's best to put your altar away and try another time again. Otherwise, look for the perfect spot on your altar for each of the items listed above, and make sure they're all facing the appropriate direction and are correctly placed to allow your spell to be as effective as possible.

How to Maintain an Altar

When it comes to altar maintenance, there are a few simple rules you should follow as guidelines. First of all, make sure that your incense is replaced every time you use it so that the same smells aren't present from one spell to another. This will make it harder for spirits to find you.

Secondly, keep all of the rest of the tools on your altar clean and tidy at all times. This may mean washing them with soap and water or polishing their surface every time you've finished using them. If they're not kept presentable, then you may find that you don't have as much control over them as you should.

It is also important to replace your candles every so often so that the wax doesn't grow stale and lose its power. As your candle dries out, it will be increasingly more difficult to use it for spell-work until it is finally burned out or damaged through age. In some cases, the wick will become flimsy and won't provide enough fire to make your spells work properly.

Finally, use a toothpick or cloth to dust off your elemental representations of water, air, earth, and fire, whenever you've finished with them for the day. This prevents dirt from building up that could cause an imbalance in your altar's elements and make it harder for you to work with them in the future.

Fire magic is one of the most powerful types of magic you can perform, but it's only powerful when it's done safely. That means having your altar set up properly before you begin any work and making sure that everything on the surface is sparkling clean at all times. Keep these four rules in mind as a guideline to make sure you're always safe during your magic, and there's nothing you can't accomplish.

In addition, make any necessary repairs or replace anything damaged on your altar as soon as possible so that it always looks its best. If you use your altar more than once a day, don't forget to clean it between uses so that no residue from one spell interferes with the results of another.

Sweep all dirt and dust off your altar every night before you go to bed to remove any unwanted energy or elements that may have been collected during the day. This will prevent them from interfering with your magic or attracting any unwanted spirits before you have a chance to deal with them.

As long as you follow these basic rules, your altar can remain stable and focused for years without any trouble at all. Keep in mind that it's a piece of furniture and should be treated as such to ensure that it lasts for as long as possible.

Don't forget to consecrate all of your tools on the altar before you use them, to remove any unwanted energy from an item by shaking it three times while holding it at arm's length. Always make sure that a candle is blown out after you complete a spell so that it doesn't interfere with your next one. When you've finished using your altar, remember to thank the elements for their help before disassembling it and putting everything back where it belongs.

At this point, you should have a good idea of how to set up your altar so that it's as safe as possible to use in fire magic. Keep these rules in mind, and you should be able to use an altar for many years without any problems or concerns.

Chapter 4: Fire Crystals, Plants, and Herbs

Fire magic consists of raw, undiluted power and is not considered for small, weak spells and incantations. It's both a dangerous and powerful element that can create and destroy. There's nothing calm or soothing about fire and it's an element that adds a transformational power to your magic. As you know, the fire element represents extreme energy, and when added to spells and rituals it can have an astounding effect.

Fire crystals and herbs were extensively used by the Celtic people and are still an essential component in Celtic cultures and rituals. The Celtic culture and rituals have evolved tremendously over the years, but the primary essence remains the same. They use natural elements to cleanse, heal, banish, and transform negative energies. Fire magic can be a catalyst for anger and love, passion and lust, banishment and purifying, and transformational spells.

Throughout the history of Wicca and magic traditions, crystals, plants, and herbs have held a special relevance and can't be replaced by any other magic elements. While crystals are used for spiritual and mental healing and rituals, plants and herbs make up essential components in physically healing fire magic rituals that take place in Celtic witchcraft.

Fire Crystals

The earliest references mentioning the use of crystals for healing and other rituals were in the Greek and Roman traditions. Celtic rituals and Irish traditions, which are closely related, also made extensive use of crystals, gemstones, and precious rock. Particularly, spell work and meditation rituals can be enhanced significantly with the use of fire crystals. However, it should be noted that fire crystals work best when combined with spells related to extreme emotions and healing. They can be used in the form of plain crystals, amulets, or other jewelry. Every spell and ritual is different and therefore requires the crystal to be used in a unique way. Fire crystals, in particular, are used to ramp up your power and energy, purify your soul, strengthen your will, and awaken your enthusiasm.

The Healing Properties of Fire Crystals

From a mythological point of view, fire was stolen by Prometheus from the gods and given to humanity in an attempt to end their suffering. It was a source of brightness and comfort, and it brought humans out of the darkness. Metaphorically, fire was used to banish the fear and hopelessness felt by humans, and so, fire magic deals with spells and rituals of a similar purpose. The healing properties of fire crystals can include:

- Cleansing your aura, especially one with excessive negative energy.
- Improving the flow of healing energy and chi through parts of your body that feel blocked or stagnant.
- Enhancing extreme feelings like passion, will, determination, and a sense of purpose.

- Fighting against psychic attacks and cutting off unwanted psychic attachments.
- Reducing negative feelings of depression, anxiety, hopelessness, or apathy.
- Channeling your emotional energy and reconnecting with emotions.
- Reinforcing your self-esteem and gaining clarity regarding your personal power.

Crystals That Channel Fire Element Energy

While there are many ways you can use fire crystals in your fire magic and witchcraft, the best way to incorporate them into your spells is to wear them on a daily basis or place them in your dominant hand when meditating. You can also use them during healing crystal sessions by placing them over the solar plexus chakra. There are numerous crystals that are best to channel the energy of fire elements, some of them are mentioned below.

1. Citrine

Citrine comes in different crystal forms, and natural and heat-treated citrine or market citrine are said to channel powerful fire element energy. These crystals are full of positive vibes, creative and warm energies that help to uplift spirits, boost your overall well-being, and improve your creative and passionate energy. Because of its yellowish gold color, it's also commonly known as the merchant's stone. In addition to its healing properties, it's said to improve communication, especially for businessmen, and it is said to attract wealth. It is generally thought of as a joyous stone, brightening the lives of people who regularly associate with it. From a physical health perspective, Citrine gemstones are said to relieve backaches and any problems related to the liver, spleen, or digestive system.

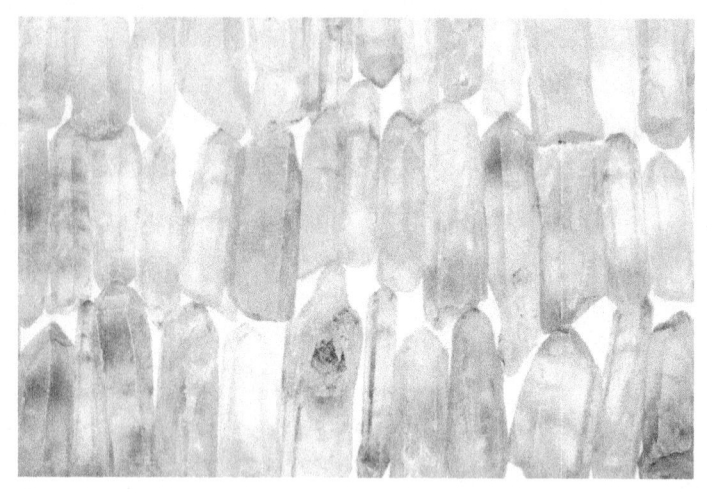

https://unsplash.com/photos/yellow-ice-cream-cone-lot-ppmiXmhHHyc

Citrine

2. Sunstone

One of the most commonly known fire crystals, sunstone is a feldspar crystal that has a warm, translucent look. It's a crystal that represents abundance and joy; it is said to harness the sun's power to provide light when you're shrouded in darkness. By keeping a sunstone fire crystal close to you, you'll not only ensure good luck but will also be filled with positive energy throughout your day. The sunstone is like a mini-sun for those dark rainy days, whether literally or metaphorically. Its physical healing properties can include easing pain—cramps, joint pain, or any digestive system issues. It also gives you a boost of much-needed vitamin D. Similar to Citrine, sunstone crystals connect to the sacral chakra as well as the heart chakra and help form healthy relationships.

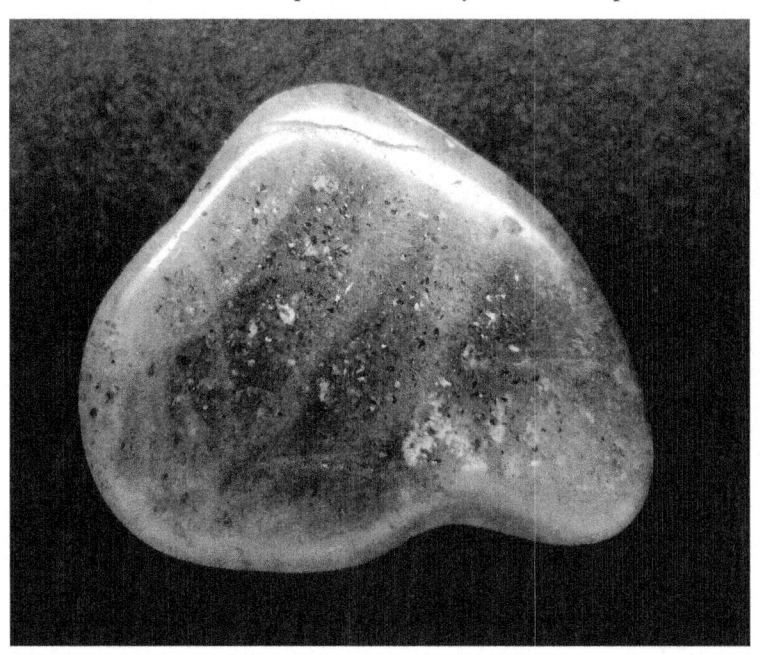

Ra'ike (see also: de:Benutzer:Ra'ike), CC BY 3.0 https://creativecommons.org/licenses/by/3.0 via Wikimedia Commons https://commons.wikimedia.org/wiki/File:Oligoclase-Sunstone_from_India2.jpg

Sunstone

3. Spessartine Garnet

Spessartine garnet is a rare fire crystal, which, when illuminated, shows off shades of red, dark gold, and orange, representing what a fire crystal should essentially look like. This crystal vibrates at intensive energies and spreads positive and encouraging energy through a person. It's also said to enhance the brain's rational thinking and problem-solving capabilities and stimulate the creative ability of an individual. As for its physical healing properties, spessartine is considered to be physically healing for the reproductive and digestive systems. Moreover, people suffering from nightmares can keep this gemstone under their pillows before sleeping to help reduce unease and anxiety. It's also said to significantly reduce depression and helps replace frequent antidepressants.

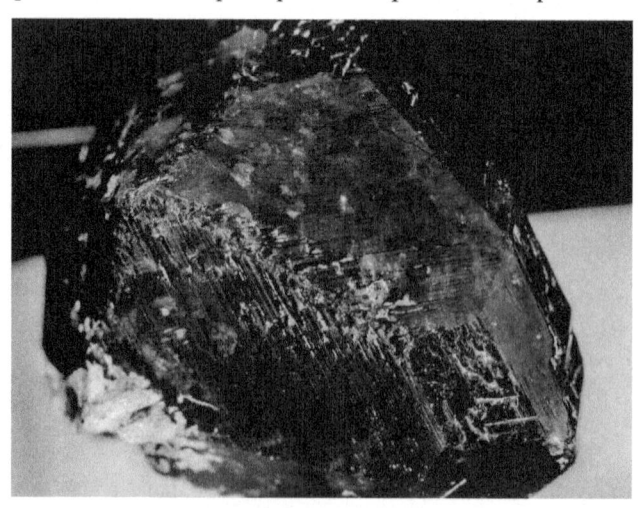

ButtShark, CC0, via Wikimedia Commons
https://commons.wikimedia.org/wiki/File:Garnet_-_Spessartine_crystal_detail.jpg

Spesartine garnet

4. Labradorite

Labradorite is a fire crystal that aligns your soul with change and transformation and helps clarify life's purpose. It's a crystal that provides power, knowledge, wisdom, and hope. Considered a tremendously spiritual gemstone, labradorite creates a shield around your aura and protects you from negative energy and people, especially from sorcery. It's also said to temper the negativity within a person and helps enhance willpower and self-esteem. This crystal connects to the throat and heart chakra, which is why it forms a protective shield around a person.

https://unsplash.com/photos/oval-blue-and-black-accessory-on-white-surface-kHrrHMMG-ME

Labradorite

5. Orange Calcite

Orange calcite is considered to be a highly therapeutic crystal as it's a crystal that provides a fresh surge of energy. Calcite is sometimes called the stone of amplification and is said to enhance your creative expression, remove negative feelings, and nurture healthy emotions. Similar to other fire crystals, it connects to the sacral chakra and helps maintain a positive outlook. With its popping orange shade and gentle aura, orange calcite can help clear any sort of emotional blockages. This crystal is said to work best for people who overwork themselves, as it helps restore energy.

https://pixabay.com/photos/calcite-orange-calcite-orange-3588062/

Orange calcite

6. Carnelian

One of the most visually appealing fire crystals, carnelian crystals are reddish-brown in color and truly represent the colors of the fire element. Considered a potent healing crystal, it has mental, physical, and spiritual healing properties all combined in one. Similar to many other fire stones, a carnelian crystal infuses your body with light, life, and hope. It also boosts fertility and enhances sexual energy. In addition, it can help people struggling with addiction issues considerably. It will also positively affect your mental health by providing a surge of positive energy, which will help you get back on your feet. Carnelian crystals are connected with the lower three chakras, i.e., the root, sacral, and heart chakra. You can use this gemstone in the form of jewelry or an ornament for your altar.

Image by Jarno https://creativecommons.org/licenses/by/2.0/
https://www.flickr.com/photos/25326737@N00/177995017

Carnelian

7. Moldavite

One of the best fire crystals for transformative rituals, moldavite is known for its ability to influence rapid changes in a person's life. It essentially clears any blockages, whether literal or metaphorical. However, one should be careful before making too much use of this rock, as a sudden change can be overwhelming for many people. Moldavite rock helps awaken your sense of purpose in life, connect with your physic abilities and activate hidden talents. It connects with the heart and sacral chakra like many other fire crystals.

James St. John, CC BY 2.0 https://creativecommons.org/licenses/by/2.0 via Wikimedia Commons https://commons.wikimedia.org/wiki/File:Moldavite_(Miocene,_14.5-14.8_Ma;_Ries_Impact_Crater%27s_tektite_strewn_field,_Bohemia)_2.jpg

Moldavite

Fire Plants and Herbs

If you're familiar with witchcraft basics, the Wiccan or Celtic traditions, and basically any spell work, you'll be aware of the importance of using the correct herb for a ritual. Herbs, incense, and spices, when combined with fire magic, can create a powerful effect. There are numerous varieties of plants and herbs that are used in fire magic to enhance rituals or the effect of spell work. Special herbs, when added to spell work or rituals, can help to purify and consecrate negative energies.

Attributes of Fiery Herbs and Plants

While there are many different types of herbs and plants available, and it's important to understand where and how each of them can be incorporated into spells and rituals, you should first be able to identify fire herbs based on certain attributes and properties. This will make it easier for you to remember and recognize fire herbs and use them efficiently in your fire magic practice. Here are some common attributes of fire magic herbs and plants.

1. Survives in Peak Sunlight

Plants and herbs that can survive scorching sunlight should be automatically assumed to be related to fire magic. Herbs that are sun-loving and tropical are almost always included as fire herbs. Examples can include rosemary, sunflower, copal, and palm plants.

2. Pungent

Herbs associated with fire are usually strong-smelling and have a relatively higher spice factor than usual herbs. Whether they have barely noticeable pleasant smells or strong obnoxious smells, fire herbs are used in spells for banishment and protection. Plus, you might have heard of the use of spicy herbs to speed up the process of a ritual or spell. Examples of this type of attribute can include cinnamon, chili, pepper, cloves, and ginger.

3. Resembles the Sun or Fire

Fiery plants and herbs are often recognized simply from their physical appearance. Plants associated with fire can have the visual appearance of the sun or fire, i.e., they are in shades of red, orange, or gold. Yellow-colored flowers can sometimes be included in the category of fiery herbs as well. Amaranth, dragon's blood, calendula, and sagebrush are all examples of fire herbs that are similar to the fire element in appearance.

4. Irritates the Skin

Fire magic is extremely powerful, and, as such, you should use herbs that are fiery in nature as well. Plants and flowers that burn or sting when coming in contact with human skin are said to be included as fiery herbs and plants. A tradition surrounding this type of plant is the use of stinging and burning plants for warding spells. Examples can include holly, mace, stinging nettle, and cedar.

5. Considered to Be Protective

Some herbs that don't have the glaring signs of being fiery plants are still considered to be in this category and are said to be especially blessed by the gods. Consequently, these herbs are used in protection spells, amulets, and protective charms. These plants are added to a ritual to create a barrier against evil, ward off negative energies and simultaneously remove the negative energy already in your space. Examples of this type of plant can include basil, angelica, cinquefoil, and wood betony.

Fire Element Herbs

For more detailed knowledge of fire herbs and plants, here is a list of details for fiery herbs and how to use them in spell work and rituals. These herbs work perfectly when added to fire magic rituals to enhance the feelings of passion, love, lust, anger, or power.

(Be sure not to ingest any of the mentioned plants or herbs unless you're 100% sure about their non-toxicity or that you aren't allergic. It's important to follow proper safety procedures when working with herbs, as allergies can go from simple to severe in just a matter of seconds.)

1. Amaranth

- **Gender:** Female.
- **Planet:** Saturn.

- **Uses:** Can be used as a protective charm or talisman.

- Also known as the flower of immortality, it can be used in healing spells, invisibility, summoning spirits, and protection against bullets.

- Carry around if you want to mend a broken heart.

- Also used in pagan burial rituals.

https://unsplash.com/photos/red-and-purple-flowers-on-brown-woven-basket-_TgBDmO-9Wg

Amaranth

2. Angelica

- **Gender:** Male.

- **Planet:** Sun.

- **Uses:** Can be used as a perfume or as a charm.

- Considered to be a powerful herb for protection, angelica is usually used to create a barrier against negative energy and protect an area.

- Can be sprinkled in your shoes for extra strength and energy.

- Can be burned if you want to get an old lover back.

- It can also be used for meditation purposes.

- Has a general effect of positivity on the user and removes any curses or hexes.

3. Ash

- **Gender:** Male.
- **Planet:** Sun.
- **Uses:** Can be used as a talisman/charm.

- Usually used for protection spells, invincibility skills, and luck.

- For protection from drowning, carve a solar cross out of ash.

- Burn an ash tree at Yule season for prosperity throughout the year.

- For safety, while traveling, the leaf of the ash tree should be carried.

4. Basil

- **Gender:** Male.
- **Planet:** Mars.
- **Uses:** Can be used as a talisman or charm.

- Basil works in spells for wealth, prosperity, love, and protection.

- Can be used in dangerous situations; carry basil with you for added courage and determination to move forward.

- Sprinkle basil outside your business associations for success.

https://unsplash.com/photos/macro-photography-of-green-leafed-plant-KSJm1IOKLBU

Basil

5. Cedar

- **Gender:** Male.
- **Planet:** Sun.
- **Uses:** Can be used as an incense/perfume.
- Cedar is considered a sacred herb to the druids and was used to bring power, money, strength, healing, and purification to an individual.
- To attract wealth, carry a small piece of this herb in your wallet, or wrap it around your money.
- Burn cedar to induce psychic abilities and reduce nightmares and feelings of unease.
- Store your fire crystals in cedar boxes for maximum effect.

https://unsplash.com/photos/brown-dried-leaves-on-ground-zI84PsYBODg

Cedar

6. Damiana

- **Gender:** Male.

- **Planet:** Mars.

- **Uses:** Can be used as an incense or as a talisman and in medicine.

- This herb promotes love, lust, and psychic visions. It is often used as a sexual stimulant.

- It can be used in sex magic, tantra magic, or deep meditation.

- Note: consuming this herb can prove to be toxic to your liver, and therefore, shouldn't be ingested without caution.

7. Dragon's Blood

- **Gender:** Male.

- **Planet:** Mars.

- **Uses:** Can be used in the form of incense to increase the power of a given spell.

- Mix dragon's blood with sugar and salt and hide it in your home to create a soothing and peaceful environment.

• This herb helps with impotence and shows promising results.

• Use its ink to write down vows or sigils, or keep it with you for good luck.

Alex Proimos from Sydney, Australia, CC BY 2.0
https://creativecommons.org/licenses/by/2.0 via Wikimedia Commons
https://commons.wikimedia.org/wiki/File:Dragons_Blood_Tree_(4054489997).jpg

Dragon's Blood

8. Hawthorn

- **Gender:** Male.
- **Planet:** Mars.
- **Uses:** Can be used as a protective talisman/charm for numerous purposes.
- For protection against lightning, its leaves should be kept in a sachet.
- In Celtic rituals, hawthorns are used as decorations and increase fertility.
- Hawthorn is said to ward against depression and other negative feelings, so keep it with you throughout the day.

https://unsplash.com/photos/selective-focus-photo-of-cherries-hwi3Xs0h8eY

Hawthorn

9. Juniper

- **Gender:** Male.
- **Planet:** Sun.
- **Uses:** Can be used as an incense or a talisman.
- Carry a sprig of juniper to attract positive energy and prevent accidents.
- Grow juniper herbs around your house, especially near doors and windows, to prevent robberies.
- Wear the plant's berries on a string around your neck to attract lovers. Men can wear it to increase fertility.

https://unsplash.com/photos/blue-flowers-on-green-plant-rdZ73uMeGM0

Juniper

10. Mandrake

- **Gender:** Male.
- **Planet:** Mercury.
- **Uses:** Can be used for medicinal purposes.
- It can also be used as a protective charm.
- Place a mandrake plant on your altar for the protection of your home, or wear it around your neck to preserve good health.
- Like other nightshade plants, mandrakes are poisonous and shouldn't be ingested.

Image by Jenny Laird https://creativecommons.org/licenses/by/2.0/
https://www.flickr.com/photos/99095055@N04/22692411280

Mandrake

11. Marigold

- **Gender:** Male.
- **Planet:** Sun.
- **Uses:** Can be used as a talisman.

- Place the flower under your pillow to induce clairvoyant dreams and psychic visions.

- Carry it with you if you want to gain respect and success.

- Keep these flowers in a vase to get a surge of energy and happiness.

https://unsplash.com/photos/orange-flowers-with-green-leaves-2j8X-RpB1sM

Marigold

12. Rosemary

- **Gender:** Male.

- **Planet:** Sun.

- **Uses:** Can be used medicinally.

- To enhance your spellwork and ritual effects, burn rosemary for a cleansing smoke to remove all negativity.

- Wear or carry rosemary herbs to improve your memory and get a clear brain.

- Place under your pillow to reduce nightmares.

https://unsplash.com/photos/green-plant-on-brown-clay-pot-v5Px2pav-MM

Rosemary

13. Witch Hazel

- **Gender:** Male.

- **Planet:** Sun.

- **Uses:** Can be used medicinally and as a talisman.

- This herb can be used to treat bruises but should be dealt with cautiously.

- Carry herbs to ward off grief and depression.

https://unsplash.com/photos/yellow-and-brown-leaves-in-tilt-shift-lens-O5cU4iGQg3o

Witch Hazel

Don't Forget About Fire Safety!

It's easy to get caught up in the mesmerizing and powerful process of fire magic and rituals and forget about the fire prevention cautions that need to be taken. A spell or ritual consists of various elements, many of which can be highly flammable. Therefore, caution is extremely necessary to ensure no accidents happen. Your altar may have plants and herbs placed close to candles, which is an obvious fire hazard. So, you need to be extremely cautious when dealing with fire magic and flammable items and reduce the risk of a fire as much as you can. Here are some ways you can do that.

- Make sure all flammable or burnable items are placed cautiously so that they are not at risk of catching a flame and starting an unquenchable fire.

- Don't light too many candles. Although rituals have certain requirements, ensure that you don't light more candles than you need or can keep track of. A good rule of thumb is to light candles in only one area so that you can keep an eye on them.

- Ensure that you never leave a burning candle unattended. If you need to leave the room, put the flame out first.

- When burning incense, make sure you use a metal or glass holder so that there is no fire hazard.

- Learn how to use a fire extinguisher, and familiarize yourself with its functions.

- Make sure your smoke alarms are functional.

- Use LED candles as substitutes for real candles.

Chapter 5: Fire and Norse Myths

Norse mythology stresses the importance of fire and ice, the two elements which create the universe and cosmos. Fire generates, degenerates, creates, and destroys all entities, which is also an elaborate message conveyed through Norse mythology and paganism. Norse mythology tells numerous interesting stories, one of which includes the role of fire and its magic. Norse paganism is intricately connected to the fire element and draws parallels between the destruction and creation of the Norse world and the realms. Just like many cultures, fire was an important element for the Norsemen too.

Several deities and giants in the Norse world were linked to fire. The gods provided light, direction, enlightenment, whereas other giants were linked to destruction and damnation. Odin, the creator of the world, was also referred to as the god of fire. Odin, Baldur, and Loki are known as the gods of fire as they embodied similar traits and attributes. Norse mythology and paganism focused on the concept of death and resurrection, which is why the fire element was significant to the Norse world. Just like fire can create or destroy an entity, depending on the way it is handled, the Norse world was created, destroyed, and recreated by the actions of the deities and giants.

The Norse God of Trickery – Loki

Loki was a popular Norse God primarily known for his tricks and funny character. He often tricked other gods for his own benefit or just to have fun. Even though Loki did not have any qualities resembling or representing fire, he was still known as the god of fire. He could change shape, shift into creatures or beings of his choice, and change his sex as well, a quality he often used to trick other gods. He used his shapeshifting ability to attract wisdom, women, and wealth. However, he mainly used his ability as a trickster for sheer pleasure. Among all deities and living creatures in the Norse world, Loki was one of the most significant characters in their mythology (not necessarily for good deeds or nobility).

Just like fire symbolized creativity and motivation, Loki was also known for his intelligence and creativity. However, his tricks and drive often led him into trouble, particularly with the gods in Asgard. At times, he was consulted to derive plans using his trickster mind and implement new solutions to rescue Asgard. The fire and burning creativity within him portray his shared attributes with the fire element. Just like fire can be manipulated to bring illumination or destruction, Loki implemented his own will to create or destroy entities in Asgard and other realms in the Norse world.

Despite being an offspring of a giant (his father was called Fárbauti), Loki was still considered an Aesir god and stayed in the Pantheon at Asgard. At times, he wanted to create something special or take a step toward nobility, but would somehow mess it up in the end. He was inspired by Odin to do good deeds and to achieve important milestones. However, he failed every time and eventually gave up. His inner fire was ignited by anger and determination to destroy the Pantheon and the realm. He used his power to put an end to the world and pushed the universe into nothingness.

Loki enjoyed the company of Thor and Odin, the two main gods at Asgard. They often relied on Loki to devise a plan and use his creativity for the betterment of the Pantheon and the realm. However, Loki also managed to cause embarrassment and put Thor and Odin in difficult situations. According to a popular myth, Loki was jealous of Odin and his family and used his evil power to destroy everything around him. When he was in the mood to fight or trouble the gods, he entered the Pantheon and event gates uninvited and drank the beverages made for the gods. Due to his insensitivity and cynical behavior, many gods despised his presence in the Pantheon.

Loki shared several attributes with Prometheus, who was also known as the Fire God. The gods and giants assumed Loki to be on their side whereas, in reality, he never picked a side. He was neither noble nor evil. He simply used his ability to trick others and test his own boundaries. His main intention was to trouble others and he sought pleasure out of his demeaning experiences. Loki had a major hand in killing Balder, Odin's son.

According to a myth, Loki could also be attributed to the origin of cooking with fire. His name is loosely tied with the word "logi," which means fire. Some confuse Loki with Logi, the giant, and use the names interchangeably. Despite being different characters, both shared traits related to fire. During the devastating battle of Ragnarok, Loki's connection with fire signified the burning of the Norse world and the destruction of the gods. Just like the universe and realms were recreated after being burned down, we get a new edible product after cooking with fire.

The Giant of Fire and Lava – Surtr

The Fire Giant, Surtr, was a significant character of the Norse world. He was believed to be created from the first melted drops of ice along with other creatures. Surtr means "black," a name believed to have originated from his burnt or charred appearance, which came about from his connection to fire. He lived in Muspelheim (the realm of fire) and led a huge army to fight against the Vanir and Aesir gods. He was fated to kill Freyr, the god of rain, fertility, and peace. He also used a burning sword that came from the realm of fire and heat.

Surtr despised the Aesir and wanted to destroy them by attacking Asgard and destroying it completely. During the event of Ragnarok (the apocalypse in the end), Surtr used his flaming sword with the intention of destroying Asgard and taking revenge. During the battle, he killed the god of summer, Freyr, with his sword. Surtr is believed to be a supernatural force that resembles the Underworld volcanic fire. Surtr hid deep within Muspelheim and gathered resources to fight the gods during Ragnarok. He laid out a plan to destroy the gods and trained other giants to form an army.

Surtr was destined to die at the final battle at the hands of Odin and Thor. He was also fated to bring the flames and burn the world. Before Odin and Thor killed Surtr, he successfully burned Asgard during Ragnarok, thereby leading to the recreation of the world. Until Ragnarok began, Surtr and his army remained undercover and attacked when the gods appeared. Surtr did not mind sacrificing himself during the battle. His main aim was to destroy Asgard and the entire world to start another cycle. He spent a major part of his life honing his skills and his burning sword.

Surtr was born after his brother Ymir, when Odin and his brothers created the world. He carried a primordial flame that provided warmth to the cosmos and helped to create the stars and the sun. Essentially a magical entity known as a "jötunn," Surtr portrayed a dogmatic personality and had just one main goal which was to keep moving toward fulfilling his prophecy. He was selfless and wanted to be a part of the recreation process, even if he was meant to die. It is believed that Surtr was one of the mightiest and most powerful giants, second only to his brother, Ymir. Due to his burning passion, fiery nature, and constant training, Surtr could fight Thor and Odin.

Some records state that Surtr was destined to be immortal. He lived in Muspelheim for centuries from the time of his birth. His superhuman strength and stamina made him superior to the other giants and creatures among all nine realms in Norse mythology. Since he was born during the creation of the burning red-hot realm of Muspelheim, Surtr also gained immense endurance. Despite staying awake all night and day, he had boundless stamina that allowed him to stand against the Asgard gods and fight with vigor.

Surtr created his own weapon from fire, which made it one of the strongest attacking and defending tools in the Norse world. Surtr's weapon was so powerful that it could overcome the Blades of Chaos and Mjölnir's weapon as well. Surtr was often compared to the "Titan of Destruction," Perses. Every breath released by Surtr contributed to the creation of the cosmos. Even though he lost and died in the battle, the giant played a significant role in the creation of the universe.

The Giant of Fire – Logi

As mentioned, Logi, the fire giant, is often confused with Loki, the trickster God. Despite being barely mentioned in major Norse accounts, Logi is still well-known for his personification of fire. In Prose Edda, Logi is named "Gylfaginning." One of the most famous accounts representing the fire giant tells the story of his participation in an eating contest. He competed against Loki, who was also determined to win. They were presented with a table full of meat. Whoever finished it was the winner. Since Loki liked to eat and was proud of his eating skills, he was prepared to beat Logi. However, Loki's pride was stomped over by Logi's supremacy. The fire giant ate the meat, bones, and every morsel that was laid out on the table. He even gobbled the wood platter that was used to present the food. By contrast, Loki ate just the meat, thereby losing to the giant.

Some accounts state that Logi was the one who essentially challenged Loki at the eating competition. Logi's father was Fornjótr (the frost giant also known as "Mistblindi"), and his siblings were Kári (Ruler of the North Wind), Gymir, Laufey, and Ægir (King of the Sea). The famous eating contest took place in Utgard, where he was appointed to serve the realm under Loki's supremacy. His might, passion, and vigor were apparent and inspired others in the realm. Since both Loki and Logi possessed burning desire and fire within them, they were competitive by nature and often competed against each other.

Logi married Glut, who bore him two daughters, Eisa (Embers) and Einmyria (Ashes). After a few years, Logi was left alone in Muspelheim as his wife and daughters died. He lived in a dark cave in the burning realm for years. Some accounts say that the giant in Muspelheim was just an archetypal character of Logi. It is believed that the myths surrounding Logi existed even before the myths of the Norse gods (the Aesir and the Vanir) were narrated. This group of three siblings—Kari, Logi, and Aegir—represent the three important elements of Sea, Fire, and Wind.

God of Knowledge – Odin

Odin possessed the fire of knowledge and wisdom. He had a burning passion for collecting and spreading knowledge, thereby making him one of the primordial gods of fire. It is believed that Odin had a significant role to play in the development of Asgard, where the Aesir gods lived. He used his knowledge to develop his realm and bring peace to the residents. Even though Odin did not display tangible aspects related to fire, the intangible fire and burning desire within him helped him gain immense knowledge. He built a throne in the sky to observe his realm and govern it with scrutiny. Huginn and Muninn, two of Odin's companions, helped him rule the realm and were also able to bring messages from the other worlds.

Odin was also known as the god of poets and the great magician. He was illustrated as a wise, old man with one eye and a long, white beard. Odin, along with his siblings, Vili and Vé, created Midgard by killing Ymir. This gave him the title of the "Allfather." Over time, he also created Asgard, where the Aesir started living. The Aesir were ruled by Odin.

Yggdrasil, the sacred tree that housed the nine realms around it, possessed a well at its roots, which was guarded by Mimir. The well was located in the Jotunheim realm. It was believed that even a single drop from the well could provide immense knowledge to the one who drank it. On discovering this, Odin embarked on a journey to find this well and drink the wisdom potion. He disguised himself as an old man wearing a hat and a blue coat. He dressed as simply as possible to avoid standing out and attracting attention.

As Odin approached Mimir and the well, he demanded to drink the water. He was ready to pay a hefty price for a single sip. Mimir asked Odin to give one of his eyes in exchange for a sip from the well. Odin had to pluck out one of his eyes and drop it into the water for the well to acknowledge his sacrifice. Without hesitating, Odin removed his right eye, grunting in pain. He dropped it into the water and Yggdrasil acknowledged Odin's sacrifice by rustling its leaves and swaying in the breeze.

Mimir filled his horn, Gjallarhorn, with the water and gave it to Odin, who then devoured every sip. This is how Odin received immense wisdom and became known as the "one-eyed god." After finishing the drink, Odin had visions and started seeing the future. Despite having just one eye, Odin saw everything clearly. In the beginning, he was unable to describe his insights and visions or illustrate them in images. The visions he had were more intense than he had ever imagined, which is why he took some time to ponder his decisions. Odin was passionate about his desire to rule and govern other Aesir gods in Asgard.

Fire of Hope – Balder

Balder was Odin and Frigg's son and was known for his just and unbiased character. He carried the fire of hope and wanted to bring justice to his people. He was compassionate, patient, and beautiful. However, he was fated to die at the hands of Loki, who, after stealing the Book of Fate, painted his future in it. Balder was well-respected and liked by his devotees. He earned the respect of other gods as well. Just like fire provides warmth and illumination to people on dark and cold nights, Balder acted as a ray of hope for people in need.

Balder also possessed the power of conjuring food and objects of his choice. He was also well-known for his act of Pyrokinesis that allowed him to create fire and throw it toward Hercules and other Olympian gods. Unlike other gods, who were skeptical about healing men on earth, Balder took the plunge and healed everyone in pain. He possessed all kinds of weapons needed to protect him against evil forces. The only thing that made him vulnerable was a poisonous arrow made from Dahak blood. Balder's bravery, possessions, and unbiased character made him one of the most significant characters of Norse cosmology.

The Norse Realm of Fire – Muspelheim

Among all nine realms of Norse mythology, Muspelheim (also known as "Múspell" in Old Norse) was known as the realm of lava, heat, and fire. Surtr, the Fire Giant, ruled Muspelheim, and all the fire giants resided in Muspelheim. This realm is believed to have originated alongside Niflheim, the realm of mist and fog, and according to the main Norse myth, the ice in Niflheim was melted by fire from Muspelheim, which gave birth to the cosmos. Muspelheim was filled with fire, sparks, flames, and lava, which made it an extremely hot realm to live in.

The melted ice from Muspelheim's warm air also gave birth to Ymir, who was the father of all giants. The resultant sparks and ashes turned into the Moon, the Sun, and the stars. Hvergelmer, the main well in Niflheim, is the source of multiple rivers flowing in different directions, which are Gunnthrá, Hrid, Svöl, Ylgr, Fimbulthul, Fjörm, Sylgr, Gjöll, Víd, and Slidr. Collectively, they formed the "Élivágar" or "Elivog." Over time, the rivers spread across different parts of the realm and reached inaccessible points. Some parts of the rivers contained venom, which is why the realm was completely turned into ice and frost.

As the warm air and heat from Muspelheim started spreading, the ice evaporated and turned into rain. Over time, the water from the rain turned into rime. The water and rime were then directed toward Ginnungagap, which was the primordial void. As the void collected multiple layers of ice, the northern part was filled with thick, crusted frost. The inner part collected storms, whereas Ginnungagap's southern part brought up warm air and fire sparks from Muspelheim. Over time, Ginnungagap was taken over by the nine realms of Norse mythology.

According to modern myths, Muspelheim can be compared to hell, which is also the Devil's home. Sinners who are directed toward hell face a hard time and burn to pay for their evil deeds. They are then left to survive in darkness, heat, and horror for eternity. Named Helheim, it is the realm of the dead who get enclosed within the gates of hell. Collectively, both realms represent hell, as illustrated in modern Christianity. Due to the presence and rule of Surtr, people were afraid to enter Muspelheim.

Muspelheim has been illustrated and depicted as the realm of Fire in modern cinema, videogames, and pop culture as well. According to Norse men, Muspelheim was the first realm or the stepping-stone toward the creation of living creatures. Despite being "evil" or "uncomfortable," Muspelheim was, therefore, still considered as an important realm in Norse mythology. All the giants and creatures residing in Muspelheim collectively fought the Gods at Asgard, specifically during Ragnarok. Just like the other realms were broken down during the apocalyptical end, Muspelheim was destroyed too.

Chapter 6: Candle Burning Rituals

Rituals that involve burning candles have been around since candles were first invented and are still common in a myriad of different cultures and belief systems. Often performed using an array of colored candles, each color signifies something different depending on which belief system is involved. People burn candles for prayers, as well as invoking the powers of the moon and other planets when performing these rituals. This chapter focuses on candle-burning spells and how they are performed.

Purpose of Candle Burning Rituals/Magic

Candle burning dates back to the ancient Egyptians who used candles not only for light but for other purposes like prayers and rituals. Candles are still widely used in prayers and rituals today. For instance, some churches burn candles on the altar. This is not because the preacher needs light but as a symbol of power and long life. Candles are also burned at funerals to honor the dead, and at weddings to bring a happy life to the newlyweds. In all this, it's the power of the symbolism of fire that is invoked.

In some instances, candles are used to cast spells for good or evil. However, a spell is not automatically evil, since it is just an intention that is deliberately put out into the universe. When you light a candle for prayer or to seek divine intervention for your sick relative, that is considered a spell. A candle is believed to bring energy and power to affect our daily lives. The power of burning candles is evident in different cultures across the globe. Candles are used for spell casting, magic, rituals, devotions, prayers, and during meditation.

The energy produced by a burning candle is spiritual and metaphysical, although you may not understand the power of a burning candle from a scientific perspective. Another significant aspect of candle-burning rituals pertains to the color of different candles. As you are going to see in the section below, different colors of candles symbolize a number of meanings or intentions. The power of fire in the candle is believed to bring transformation. Because of this, people practice candle magic to fulfill different needs in their lives. If you want to perform some candle rituals, this guide provides you with a step-by-step approach.

What You Need to Perform Candle Rituals

The act of lighting a candle for rituals is intentional, and you should know the exact reason why you want to invoke firepower. To perform a candle ritual successfully, you need to have a number of items at hand:

- A candle—choose the appropriate type of candle and color to suit your purpose and intention.
- A pen and piece of paper.
- You can also have other items like essential oils, sage, crystals, or incense, although they may not be necessary. You can add these things if you want to make the space feel sacred.

When you have gathered all the materials you want to use in your candle magic, there are different steps you should follow.

How to Perform a Candle Ritual

When you plan a spell, it means you have started the process of casting it. More importantly, remember to keep a positive attitude and make your intentions good. The following are the steps that you can consider when you begin your journey of performing a candle ritual.

Set Your Magical Goal

The first step is to know exactly why you are performing the ritual. You need to be clear in your intended magical goal, which will outline what you want to achieve. You should write your goal in one sentence, clearly stating what you want. For instance, you may need guidance when you travel or want money to start a business. When setting your goal, bear in mind the following tips:

- Be specific—e.g. "I want to be promoted at work."
- Set a realistic goal and avoid fantasy.
- Be ethical.
- Always use positive language.
- Break bigger goals into smaller ones.

With these tips, try to write a short and precise sentence outlining your goals.

Design Your Spell

Your goal should play a crucial role in helping you design your candle magic spell. Find an appropriate chant that resonates with your goal and the belief system within which you are acting. You can obtain this online or just decide on something that aligns with your desires. Additionally, you may also check the lunar calendar and choose the ideal moon sign or zodiac sign for your spell. In some cases, spells and planetary elements share some similarities and powers that you may need to invoke as you cast your spell. Remember to use things that have meaning to your life.

Collect the Required Components

Now that you have a goal for your candle ritual, you should choose various components that align with it. You need to get an appropriate candle color, herbs, oils, spices, and any other component that aligns with that goal. The most important thing that you should consider is to choose the appropriate candle for your ritual.

There are different types of candles, but you can get any for your spell. Some of the candles you can use include tapers, pillar candles, votive candles, tea lights, and others. Choosing the right one that corresponds to your goal is a component of learning witchcraft. Depending on your specific goal, the candle's color plays a significant role in determining the outcome of your ritual.

Black Candles

Depending on your beliefs, black candles have different meanings. According to the popular view by many people, black candles are associated with black magic or other evil rituals. These candles can be used for negative forces that cause destruction. However, black candles can also be used for protection and stopping or reversing negative thoughts. The candles can conceal, create confusion, absorb, introduce a new beginning, and help people to acquire new knowledge.

https://unsplash.com/photos/brown-twigs-near-black-container-EQulcczKkwY
Black candle

In astrology, the color black is believed to be very powerful, and it denotes magic. A black candle represents patience, self-control, and endurance. Black candles also have religious purposes, meaning that they are no different from any other. In religion, a black candle can be used to mourn the death of a loved one. You can also use it when praying for something painful and deep inside your heart. It also helps you focus your thoughts and prepare you for deep meditation. Therefore, black is associated with both positive and negative meanings, so you can freely choose what you want to do with it.

White Candles

White candles are the most commonly used for aspects like cleansing since they represent purity, innocence, spiritual healing, peace, truth, clarity, and rest. White candles are believed to symbolize religion, and also act as a neutral color that represents all the colors of the rainbow. When you burn a black candle together with a white one, this will help to eliminate negativity. The color white plays a crucial role in neutralizing and purifying all the negative elements associated with something.

Yellow Candles

Yellow candles are believed to symbolize knowledge, happiness, success, confidence, quick action, prayer, and devotion. With yellow candles, you can achieve great things like passing exams, because the yellow color is associated with intelligence and logic. You can use the candle to overcome adversity and achieve great things in your life. A combination of black and yellow candles produces healing powers, and also helps you to reduce issues like depression. Yellow candles also stimulate your mind and improve your memory.

Blue Candles

Blue candles are mainly used for healing, meditation, obtaining the truth, and summoning the angels. They also represent peace, protection, health, law, court cases, joy, harmony, and kindness. If you use blue candles, you can get spiritual protection. When you use both black and blue candles, their powers are merged to work for you positively. Before you pray, you should light the two candles then ask for protection and the removal of sorrow from your heart. These two candles can make a big difference in your life.

Brown Candles

You can use a brown candle to communicate with angels, and it also influences the power of practicality and neutrality. Brown candles can also be used when seeking employment, finding lost items, pursuing justice, and helping the poor. The meanings of brown and black candles are merged when you light them, and your prayers are likely to be answered.

Purple Candles

Purple candles are known for ambition, power, mastery, business success, and wisdom. Politicians usually use purple candles to pray for luck and energy. When you light a black and a purple candle, it will bring about some positive energy while banishing bad luck. You only need a prayer to fulfill your spell.

Red Candles

Red candles symbolize energy, self-confidence, passion, love, magnetic attraction, courage, and marriage. Many people often associate red candles with passion, but this is not always the case. Black and red candles help you to overcome the negative feeling of an inferiority complex or not believing in yourself.

Gold Candles

Gold candles can be used for wealth, success, power, fast luck, prosperity, and control. If you want to achieve any of these things in life, you need to burn a gold candle together with a black candle and pray for your spell to work.

Green Candles

Green candles have their meaning embedded in growth, like plants. They also symbolize wealth, good fortune, fast luck, healing, success, fertility, beginnings, and influence generosity. When you use a black candle together with a green one, you overcome negative energy and misfortunes. Before you make a life-changing prayer, light these two candles.

Orange Candles

Orange candles denote sexual stimulation, attraction, energy, control, prophetic dreams, and change of plans in some instances. When you are going through some bad times with your partner, an orange candle together with a black one will eliminate these misfortunes. The meanings of both candles will merge to provide sexual power, and your partner will regard you passionately.

As you can see, different candle colors have different meanings, so it is up to you to choose something that will work for you. Depending on your wish or intention, any candle can be used for rituals, and you should not believe in the idea that black candles are associated with black magic, since it is not true. While you can light a single candle, it is recommended that you use two, so that people will not suspect that you are doing witchcraft.

Dress the Candle

The next step in candle-burning rituals is to dress the candle after choosing an appropriate one. When you establish the link between your goal and the candle, you must dress it for the occasion. If you have oil, this is the time to rub it onto your candle. There is no strict way to apply the oil on the candle. Just choose a method you are happy with since there is no universal way to perform this task.

You can also take this opportunity to add herbs and spices to your candle. This is optional, but herbs and spices can play a role in lending power to the spell. All you need to do is to choose spices and herbs that are compatible with your goal. Do some research about different complements you may need for your ritual.

While still at the stage of dressing your candle, you also need to visualize your intent. Your mental state is very important as you rub the oil on the candle. Remember to pour your mentality and intent into the candle for energy. You can chant if you feel that it will make a difference. You will also sense the energy building, and you can feel your hands tingling or pulsing with energy.

Another way to add power to your candle is to scratch numbers, symbols, or names in candle wax. For example, you can do this for money spells to increase your chances of achieving your desired goals. Feel free to add anything that can improve your luck. You must feel the goal before you light the candle. Therefore, make sure you properly dress your candle, and it is supercharged.

Light the Candle

When it is time to cast your spell, find the right place and light your candle. You must find an appropriate space that feels magical. It is a good idea to find an enclosed space so that the candle can burn steadily. When you are satisfied that the place is free of clutter, you can light your candles and do the following things.

Use Meditation

When you light the candle, you must use meditation to help yourself relax and get into the right frame of mind. You can achieve this by taking deep breaths while at the same time releasing tension from your body and mind. You can also use meditation to get rid of worries and other intrusive thoughts that can be affecting your vision.

You should sit on the ground in a relaxed way so that you can feel your energy descending into the earth. This can go a long way in deepening your connection with the spiritual world and the universe. Also, take some time to meditate on your intention while at the same time asking for guidance and clarity. You also need to listen to the answers.

Visualize Your Goal

You must visualize your goals and try to create a picture of how they can make a difference in your life. Try to put yourself in a position where you view your mission as if you have already accomplished it, and picture how you will use your newfound blessings to turn around your fortunes. You must always repeat your chant or affirmations when you create a clear vision in your mind. This will help you raise your energy levels and boost confidence that you will achieve whatever you want. When you feel your body bustling with energy and confidence, it means that you are going in the right direction. You must not skip any day without visualizing your goals.

Create a Positive View of Your Goals

It is critical to create a positive attitude about your goals. Try to imagine how amazing you will feel when you accomplish them. A positive attitude is also good, since it helps to remove negative thoughts that can affect your mind. Some people fail to realize their goals in life because of self-doubts.

Tell yourself that you are a winner, and this helps you to develop inner satisfaction and happiness. You will also feel relieved and relaxed when you believe that you will achieve positive results. If you anticipate positive things, your life will significantly change for the better. You need to reassure yourself that you will achieve your goals and fulfill your dreams.

Imagine the Light Aura

You must visualize the candle's light aura and how it continues to grow larger as you look at it. In your imagination, the candle's light begins small and grows as it is placed outside or in any open space. This is how your objectives will progress. Your goal may begin small, but once it is exposed to the light of day, nothing will be able to stop it from expanding. What you see in your imagination is a manifestation of how your goals will develop. If you want, you can continue with your chants to find the motivation that will keep you getting stronger. Whenever you experience something negative, you should remain committed until you achieve everything you desire.

Spend Time Visualizing Your Goal

Prayers are not always answered instantly, which means you must not stop visualizing your goals. When you ask for something through prayer, you must have faith since this is the only way you can achieve your dreams. Faith involves a positive attitude and a strong belief that you will get what you have requested from the universe. In other words, you will maintain a strong connection with the spiritual world if you spend more time visualizing your goal. Additionally, this will also give you hope, and you will never get tired while pursuing your goals. When you keep your dream alive, you get the opportunity to generate more ideas that can help you refine your goals.

Allow the Candle to Burn Out

The last step is to allow the candle to burn out in its place and do not disturb it. The candle may burn out completely, or it may just melt away. Whatever the case, leave it like that. It is also not a good idea to relight your candle once it dies down, as this will interfere with the intention that the candle represents. When your candle burns out, the next thing is to take out your written intention together with any remnants of remaining wax. Wrap these components properly, since you will plant them as you do with any type of seed in the ground. You can take a walk to find the appropriate place where you will bury your intention.

After burying your intention together with the candle remnants, you should give thanks and gratitude for the benefits you will get. You must have a positive attitude and show appreciation to the Earth for continued support. When you plant your intention, this is a way of giving back to the earth so it can continue providing blessings. It is a good idea to close your ritual with massive gratitude and blessings.

Candle burning rituals have been in existence for centuries, and they continue to flourish even up to the present day. When you want to do some candle magic, it is important to determine your true goals and buy the right candles. It is vital to use different complements to dress your candles for your rituals. While the candle is burning, you should harness various components like meditation and visualization of your goals to develop a positive attitude. The following chapter focuses on pagan fire festivals.

Chapter 7: Pagan Fire Festivals

Paganism is an umbrella term used to describe various spiritual beliefs, which developed in Europe before the advent of Christianity. Pagans are typically polytheistic, believing in multiple deities who are responsible for every aspect of life on Earth.

    The pagan fire festivals were some of the most popular events and were celebrated with bonfires and sacrifices. Each festival had a different god associated with it, and each holiday was also related to an agricultural event. When Christianity was introduced, many of the holidays were changed to Christian ones. However, some pagan elements did remain in our modern celebrations. Many pagans believe that their religion is still practiced today in the form of secret societies and other underground groups. This chapter will focus on the pagan fire festivals that were already celebrated in ancient times and will describe their meaning and how they played a role in pagan culture; and will begin by describing several festivals celebrated in Europe throughout history. It will then discuss how these pagan festivals have been adapted into today's culture and some of the prominent symbols from them that are still visible on the world stage.

Beltane

The fire festival known as "Beltane" was celebrated on May 1 and was a fertility rite marking the beginning of summer. The tradition involved building a bonfire and making offerings to deities who were thought to bring luck and abundance. Offerings included items such as crops, beans, and various types of food. This was done because it was believed that spirits inhabited these items and would be attracted to the flames and smoke produced by the fire.

In the time leading up to the fire festival, all fires were extinguished within a household or village and were then started from scratch with new flames on May 1. People also washed thoroughly before attending the festivities, as it was believed that this would help them attract good fortune. The fire was used in Beltane to bless fields and livestock, and it was said to have been a good time for marriages because of the fire's fertility powers. The fire would be carried from place to place by a group of people who were guarded against evil spirits. In modern times, the May Day celebration still exists as a festival that is celebrated throughout England and other neighboring countries. Participants still carry a maypole around with them and celebrate nature, although their traditions also include dancing and drinking.

Candlemas

The festival known as "Candlemas" is celebrated in the spring, approximately halfway between the winter solstice and vernal equinox. It has become a Christian holiday associated with the end of the Christmas period; it takes place on February 2, which was when pagan followers said their New Year began. This day marks the day when people take down decorations from trees used during the winter solstice.

Candlemas is a fire festival that incorporates burning a large log while praying to the goddess Brigid, who was known to have power over fire. This log would be lit from a candle and, once alight, thrown into a river. This represents the passing of the old year and the beginning of a new one. The main reason for the festival is to bring luck. When the tradition was carried out in a public setting, it would involve people gathering together and dancing around a large bonfire.

Samhain

The fire festival "Samhain" is the most well-known in modern times. Samhain was a celebration to mark the end of summer and the beginning of winter, which meant that crops were harvested, and livestock was brought inside for shelter. This festival ended on November 1, which was believed to be when the veil between worlds thinned enough for spirits to return home.

During this time, bonfires were built in preparation for the end of autumn. These fires had many purposes, but they mainly served to ward off evil spirits and ghosts that prowled around the world during Samhain. People also believed that disguising themselves as these creatures would allow them to travel without getting hurt or lost. This is where our modern practice of dressing up in costumes originates from.

In addition, this festival also focused on ways to contact spirits so they could provide information for the future. People would offer them food and drink so they would answer questions about what was ahead. These days, the modern Halloween festival is its equivalent and is now the largest commercial holiday in America, with over 150 million people participating each year.

Lughnasadh

This festival, also spelled as "Lammas" or "Lughnasa," was once the first festival of August. This tradition took place on August 1 and was held to celebrate the beginning of the harvest season, and all fruit-bearing plants which provided food were celebrated. The celebration involved many agricultural rituals; however, these gradually became less and less important until the tradition of Lughnasadh disappeared.

The holiday is named after the Celtic god Lugh, who was known for being a great warrior and hunter. The celebrations would include people marching in religious processions, where they would carry baskets of bread behind a priest to symbolize the rewards of hard work. It was also around this time that it became customary to kill older animals because there was no point in feeding them during the colder months.

To celebrate Lughnasadh properly, bread needed to be made. People who made this bread were revered because of all that went into it, especially since the mountain was usually barren at this time of year.

Modern celebrations of the first harvest are held by the Irish as an annual Irish cultural holiday on August 1. Parades and other gatherings commemorate the start of the holiday season attended by people of various cultures and backgrounds.

Imbolc

This festival was originally held on February 1 and 2, which generally was halfway through winter. The pagan festival of Imbolc is based on the Gaelic calendar and focuses on the beginning of springtime.

The name of this holiday means "in the belly" or "milk" because it describes how the days were starting to get longer, while also symbolizing the lactating of ewes. Animals were also coming back from their winter habitats, so they were easier to hunt and kill for food sources.

The tradition would include lighting candles and fires at the end of this day to welcome the return of springtime by using colors such as yellow, red, or white to represent each season. This day was also supposed to be a time of cleansing and purification, which is why there were so many bonfires lit at the end of winter.

Mabon

This holiday, which is based on the story of Cernunnos from Celtic mythology, celebrates the fall harvest. It occurs around mid-autumn and honors the second harvest of the year in pagan traditions. For modern pagans, this also marks a time to celebrate Mabon as a god figure.

These celebrations would include the feast of Mabon, which is believed to have been a precursor to Thanksgiving. This holiday was created for people to share food with others in their communities because it marked the beginning of winter, and they needed to store up supplies before that time came.

Celtic festivals like these are still practiced by many pagans today, especially around Halloween on October 31. Fire festivals like these are popular ways for modern pagans to celebrate the seasons and mark important dates on their calendars.

Yule

This festival is held on the longest night of the year and takes place on December 21. This pagan holiday is based on the Norse tradition that honors various gods like Odin and Thor.

The tradition includes people coming together to celebrate Yule, preparing food for their "yule goats" over an open fire. The largest part of this celebration was the lighting of the yule log, which would be burned for twelve days to help usher in the coming longer days.

Since Yule is a time to celebrate the winter solstice, it also included giving presents as a way of offering thanks to the gods for being alive. This custom eventually evolved into what we know as Christmas. Modern celebrations of Yule involve gift-giving and decorating evergreen trees because it reminds people that they should feel rejuvenated after returning home. This tradition is based on the returning life force that people get to experience after enduring the darkness of winter.

Wiccan Samhain Celebration

This holiday begins on October 31 and is based around the autumn harvest that pagans would usually perform to prepare for the upcoming winter months. This is another pagan tradition that celebrates the creation of new life by using bonfires to celebrate the end of summertime.

These fire festivals are created with many different traditions, but it's common for them to include jumping over small fires to purify people before they enter into celebrations involving the family. These customs are still practiced today within various pagan communities, but they are usually done privately, with only family members being present.

Modern Parallels

Today, these pagan fire festivals are seen in many modern celebrations. Samhain is celebrated on October 31, and in these modern times it is known as Halloween. People dress up in costumes and ask friends and neighbors to give them treats. People still build bonfires for warmth during the winter season to celebrate this tradition too. Lughnasadh has also survived into modern times as something that is celebrated by millions of people, but now as the Irish holiday known as "Lúnasa."

In addition to these well-known traditions, many modern fire festivals take place all across the globe. Some examples include the Bon Festival in Japan and Prometheia in Greece. The use of candles is also still alive today but in more sacred settings. Candles are seen to represent hope and light during times of darkness. They are often lit by religious figures or used to guide processions through sacred spaces.

Modern fire festivals symbolize a variety of things. They are a way for people to celebrate the power over fire and how it can be used to create warmth and light. Fire is also representative of purification and cleansing, which ties to its historical use in pagan ceremonies to ward off evil spirits. People also come together in modern celebrations to remember traditions that originated from pagan fire festivals, such as Samhain (Halloween) and Lughnasadh (Lúnasa).

Bon Festival

First celebrated in the 10th century, this festival is also known as the Bon Odori. It takes place every year from August 16 to 22 and ends with a final dance that is meant to be performed by people of all shapes and sizes. Anyone can join in for the ritual, which symbolizes how everyone has at least one thing in common—their humanity.

Traditions/Symbolism

This festival is meant to celebrate the spirits of one's ancestors and how they exist everywhere. People pray at a shrine that displays a picture of a family member who has passed away. This is because, according to Buddhist belief, everyone must travel through numerous cycles before attaining enlightenment.

Prometheia

A modern-day fire festival that takes place in Greece and honors Prometheus, the Prometheia is celebrated to represent when humans first learned how to use fire. The tradition began with priests who would walk into a flame four times as an act of religious purification for the ancient city that was protected by the goddess Hestia. This practice is meant to show how fire can ward off evil spirits and purify a space.

Traditions/Symbolism

Modern celebrations of this festival take place on June 20, where there are many activities for people to enjoy. These include special church services that involve lighting candles, processions with young unmarried women who carry candles, and vespers that involve jumping over fire. This tradition came from the ancient Greeks, but the symbolism behind it is meant to show how fire can ward off evil spirits and purify a space.

Candlelight Processions

A Christian celebration in which people also use lighted candles. These events take place at night during Easter where religious groups march through the streets while carrying candles. The flame is meant to symbolize the light of Jesus Christ and his resurrection while also serving as a way for people to carry on this tradition that originated from pagan celebrations in Europe.

Traditions/Symbolism

People participating in these processions visit churches before they take part in them. They then walk along streets carrying candles and stopping at different altars that bear the image of Jesus Christ. At each altar, they listen to readings which explain how Jesus was resurrected on Easter Sunday after his death.

Fire Walking

An ancient pagan tradition in which people would walk through fire without getting burned, this practice is still done today but in a slightly different way. For example, there are fire walks that have been hosted by the United States Department of Defense to show soldiers how to overcome their fears and become more confident in battle.

Traditions/Symbolism

This tradition has prevailed throughout history as a pagan ritual meant to cleanse people from negative energy or any type of pain or suffering. In modern times, it can symbolize overcoming fear and being confident in the face of danger.

Halloween

One of the most prominent fire celebrations that is still alive today is on October 31, when people celebrate Halloween. This tradition began with Celtic pagans who would light bonfires to commemorate their ancestors during a time known as Samhain.

Traditions/Symbolism

People believed that ghosts of ancestors would come back to the land of the living during this time, and they also dressed in costumes to resemble these spirits. Today, people celebrate Halloween by attending costume parties or trick-or-treating with kids wearing costumes when they go door-to-door asking for candy. The tradition of bonfires is still alive but mainly through backyard fireworks displays.

Diwali

One of the biggest Hindu festivals, Diwali, is also known as the festival of lights and celebrates the triumph of good over evil. On this day, Hindus decorate their houses with candles and lamps that are lit to symbolize Lakshmi or the goddess of wealth who brings fortune into people's homes. They also let off fireworks.

Traditions/Symbolism

While lighting these lamps as a tradition, Hindus also put on new clothes and visit people they haven't seen for a long time. People exchange gifts with loved ones and enjoy fireworks displays as well as burning candle wicks to show how good conquers evil.

Midsummer

Originating from Sweden, Midsummer marks the longest day of the year during summer. This tradition has survived throughout history in many different forms, but people today still celebrate it by lighting bonfires.

Traditions/Symbolism

People in Sweden who light these fires believe it is a tradition that wards off evil spirits and spell-casting. They also believe the fire gives them luck for the rest of the year, while it's also meant to bring good crops for the year.

Dali Torch Festival

This festival began in southwestern China during the Song Dynasty, when people used to celebrate the summer solstice. During this time, they would carry giant straw-stuffed effigies of a fox through streets so they could be burned completely, symbolizing good overcoming evil, and death being defeated by life.

Traditions/Symbolism

In the modern-day version of this celebration, people carry these torches through the streets with music playing in the background. This event is meant to show how good conquers evil and brings prosperity after a year of hardship.

Holi

Otherwise known as the festival of colors, Holi started in India around 2,000 years ago, where it originally symbolized fertility. Today, it still involves people celebrating the coming of spring with the use of vibrant colors like red powder. On this auspicious day, people burn bonfires and eat special confectionery called sweetmeats.

Traditions/Symbolism

Besides burning bonfires and eating sweets, people also enjoy doing things like spraying each other with colored powder and water. This is meant to give good luck while showing that the body's color doesn't matter but instead, it's a person's soul that defines them. At this time, people throw buckets of colored water on friends and family members to wash away their bad luck. This festival is meant to celebrate the victory of good over evil.

Afrikaburn

By far the most modern of all the festivals (2007) listed here, this event takes place in South Africa's Karoo region. During this official Burning Man fire celebration, people create a large bonfire and burn an effigy of a wooden man known as "The Man," which represents evil being defeated by good.

Traditions/Symbolism

Before lighting it on fire, people chant to this effigy. During the festival, people dance around the bonfire while music plays in the background. People also drink beer and eat food at this time. For some, this event is about celebrating life, but for others, it's a safe place to let go of their emotional baggage.

Up Helly Aa

This event takes place in Scotland, where young men are dressed up as Vikings to mark the end of the yule festival. During this time, they carry torches and march through town while blowing bagpipes. Afterward, there is a huge bonfire burning high enough for people to stand inside of it.

Traditions/Symbolism

The torch-lit parade, the large bonfire that is lit, and the burning of a replica Viking longboat all symbolize the Norse god Odin riding through Asgard on his eight-legged horse Sleipnir. This time also marks the end of winter after six long months. The replica Viking ship that's burned represents all the bad things people want to leave behind in the past. This celebration is meant to show that good overcomes evil and brings life after death.

Fire festivals are some of the most interesting events that have been celebrated by different cultures throughout history. Among these are holidays like Beltane, Samhain, and Lughnasadh. They're meant to celebrate fertility or harvests after a long winter while banishing bad luck. It also seems that fire is very symbolic during these times, whether it's meant to purify you or bring life back after death.

In the end, it seems that fire festivals are about celebrating life and overcoming death. Whether you're part of a pagan, Christian, Hindu, or any other tradition, fire is an important symbol in many ways. It's used to ward off evil spirits while also bringing good luck for the new year ahead. Fire is also seen as a purifying force by some cultures because it can be wielded against darkness. The modern-day versions of these celebrations may vary, but they all have one thing in common, they celebrate light triumphing over darkness and hope for better times on the horizon.

Chapter 8: Performing Fire Spells Safely

Fire spells play a pivotal role in helping people from different backgrounds perform elemental magic. However, fire comes with several risks, which can include property damage, serious injuries, or even death in worst-case scenarios. Likewise, there are specific safety precautions and common sense that you must take into account when working with fire, which includes the correct safety equipment. As such, this chapter discusses the measures you should take when practicing your magic to become a better fire witch.

Fire Safety Tips You Should Know

Fire spells can be very powerful and offer you many positive things in life. Depending on the method you use to cast your spells, you can get spiritual protection, emotional stability, and good health. However, you need to exercise caution while performing fire spells, not only when you are casting them, but also in your intention and the physical manifestation of the rituals.

Do Not Harm Anyone

You should always remember the Wiccan Rede, which clearly states that you can do what you want as long as you do not harm anyone. This statement is rich advice and must guide you in whatever you do concerning fire spells. It encourages you to take personal responsibility for your actions. You must always keep your intentions simple, clear, and clean so that you do not cause harm to other people. If you are certain that a fire spell will yield positive results in your life, you must be kind enough to consider other people's safety needs.

Avoid Manipulating Others

You should avoid casting spells that aim to manipulate other people. This is a sequel to the first rule, and it states that you may be causing harm to someone if you try to change their behavior against their will. In other words, you should not use your fire spells to try to influence or change other people's behaviors or their minds. You can cause harm in the process, and this will be against the essence of spells. To avoid negative effects, you should state that your spell must not harm anyone.

Seek Consent First

You should avoid a scenario where you cast spells on behalf of other people without seeking their consent. This is not safe, since your witchcraft can negatively impact the individuals involved. When you think your spells can help others, make sure you perform them responsibly and let them know what you intend to do before you start. In short, you must get their permission. This is an important aspect of performing fire magic, as, even with the best intentions in the world, the person you are trying to help might not share your belief system and could be highly offended that you are trying to impose your ideas on them. It is a good idea to let those individuals interested in your spells approach you instead of imposing your spiritual beliefs on them.

Maintain Privacy

You should always try to keep your spells private to ensure total safety. Once you share your intentions with other people, they may not come true. Additionally, sharing your spiritual matters can attract backlash from other groups, and you can also be persecuted. You should not boast about specific spiritual practices to other people who have not asked you to share such details. This can compromise your fire spells since the outcome may not meet your expectations.

If you tell other people your spellwork, their thoughts and feelings may interfere with the outcome. They could be a part of another belief system diametrically opposed to yours. Therefore, it is always a noble idea to perform your magic in a safe and private place where there is no interference. You can only share your work with the witches that you trust.

Protect the Environment

Always make sure that you protect nature when you perform your fire spells. If you leave your fire unattended, it can get out of hand and end up destroying the environment. You should also consider using biodegradable tools and materials when you conduct your spellcasting works. This can go a long way toward reducing your carbon footprint. You also need to be conscious about how you dispose of the remnants from your rituals. When you practice some magic outdoors, make sure you clean up after yourself and dispose of everything properly that can affect Mother Nature. Ethically sourced and organic products are safe for your fire spells, since they do not cause as much harm to the environment.

Practice Fire Safety

Practicing fire safety is the crux of this chapter, and it involves several things. If you intend to cast candle spells, you must get a sturdy candle holder. And because you are using candles, you are literally playing with fire and should use common sense when it comes to where you place your candles. You must avoid placing your candles close to windows with curtains and blinds, since they can easily catch fire. Make sure your candle is free from clutter and other flammable materials. More importantly, do not leave the burning candle unattended. When you want to leave the candle burning continuously, make sure you place it in a sink, metal tray, enclosed glass container, or a basin with water.

Stay Protected

You must perform regular cleansing to ensure that you stay protected. You can also ensure safety by cleaning your home and workplace regularly. Cleaning your body will ensure your safety by protecting you against psychic attacks and other negative energies that may affect your welfare. You also need to take good care of your body so that it is in good health. No amount of magic can substitute quality medical care.

Use the Right Tools

Whenever you decide to perform fire spells, you must use appropriate tools and equipment. You must also do it in the right frame of your mind to ensure that everything goes well. You need the following supplies when performing fire spells:

- Candle.
- Piece of paper.
- Lighter or match.

Candles

Candles play a critical role since they are used for many spell purposes. Make sure you choose the appropriate candle in the first place. There are different types of candles available on the market, so your ultimate choice is a matter of personal preference. You must dress your candles, such as with herbs and oils. To ensure safety, make sure all the elements you use are not harmful. Other items can be hazardous to the environment, so prioritize ethical sourcing.

Fluorescent light is another option you can consider when performing fire spells safely. This is the most common light used in homes. When performing spells, fluorescent light can provide the same benefits that you can get from candles. It is strongly believed that fluorescent light illuminates a situation, lights the way, or provides a steady source of energy to a spell. This is a safer way of casting spells, since the source of light does not pose any risk of a fire outbreak that can destroy property or cause injuries to different people.

A Bowl

If you want to perform an ancient fire spell when you use a burning candle, you must get a bowl or any container that can be filled with sand or water. The fire bowl you can use for indoor fire magic must not be very big, but it should be made of brass or enamel. Choose material that will prevent the candle from burning the table. Another important thing that you should do is to place the bowl holding the burning candle in a safe place away from flammable objects.

When you start performing your fire spells, make sure you won't activate a smoke detector if you have one. Smoke detectors are highly recommended to keep you safe from any unexpected fires in your home. You can also open a window, as long as it will not disturb the candle. The idea of opening a window is that it will provide an escape route for the smoke coming from the candle so that it goes to heaven. If you are burning different types of herbs, they can produce thick smoke, so there should be proper ventilation in your home.

The other safer way of casting your fire spell is to use little pieces of twigs from specific trees, which can burn easily. You must experiment with different types of woods to get the right flavor of smoke. Whatever you choose to burn, try to find something that is as environmentally friendly as possible. There are various herbs you can get from your garden or local grocery store.

Different pieces of wood allow you to make a small fire inside the bowl. The advantage of a small fire is that the flames can burn out quickly under your watch, so they may not pose any danger to your property. You will be left with embers when the fire goes out, and this is the time you can add herbs to produce powerful smoke to use for your prayers.

Hearth Fire

Apart from lighting a candle, hearth fire is another well-known method of casting fire spells. Hearth fires are usually associated with warmth, wellness, health, creativity, wisdom, and life. This option consists of a stove or a fireplace that is commonly used for cooking or providing warmth when it is cold. When you choose this option to cast your spells, make sure the fireplace is located in a central position inside the kitchen or living room.

You should use charcoal in your hearth if you want to cast spells. Charcoal consists of burnt remains of coal, firewood, or other types of organic materials. Charcoal is good for purification, cleansing, and banishing. It also offers great protection against evil spells. Since charcoal mainly consists of glowing embers, it is a safe way of performing your spells. Glowing embers do not pose as much danger since they are indoors and cannot be blown by the wind. This means that you can safely use charcoal for your rituals. The embers will slowly die without causing harm, as long as they stay undisturbed in the hearth or stove.

Other Safe Methods of Performing Fire Spells

There are other substitutes to fire that you can consider for your spell. As long as there is a source of heat other than fire, you can safely perform your rituals. Other sources of energy are safer than fire, and they give you peace of mind, since you are not worried about issues like injuries or property damage. All you need to do is to choose the best method that suits your needs when you perform your spells. Other sources of energy are easy to get, and they can save you time and money. The following are some of the safe methods you can consider for your fire spells.

Sunlight

Sunlight is the Earth's major source of fire energy. It warms the atmosphere, provides life, allows plants to grow, and provides energy for different processes that enhance the Earth. Sunlight can also be used for purification, charging, energizing, and cleansing. Energy from the sunlight is generally good for many purposes. You can also use sunlight to illuminate or ignite a situation and to remove negativity.

Sunlight is a renewable source of energy that does not cause any carbon footprint on the environment. In other words, it is the safest form of power if you want to perform fire spells. When you consider this method, you do not burn anything, since you will only use natural light that is also free. You only need to be careful not to get sunburnt when you do your spells. With this method, there is no fear of causing fire outbreaks that can damage property. However, timing is crucial when you choose to use sunlight for your spells.

Sunflower

Sunflower is a unique flower that follows the sun all day long, and it also looks like the sun. A sunflower symbolizes joy, fertility, warmth, and good luck. You can use a sunflower when you perform your fire spells since it can substitute artificial fire. This is a very safe method that does not cause any bodily harm or pose risks to the environment. This natural remedy does not leave any footprint on the environment.

Tin

Tin has a close link with Jupiter, which symbolizes lightning. Therefore, you can use the tin to invoke lightning or protect against it. This type of material is supercharged during a storm with lightning, and this makes it a potent magical material. You can use the tin to give you what you desire, and it is perfect for success in spells. When you choose this option, no harm is caused, and everyone will be very safe.

However, you need to be careful since a bolt of lightning can be very dangerous if it catches you unaware.

Rainbow

Rainbows are formed by the light that passes through the prism created by water droplets. Rainbows symbolize joy and hope and they are believed to act as a bridge between different worlds. You can use rainbows to communicate with the dead, connect with the supernatural world, and inspire hope. As a result, this is a good alternative for performing your fire spells. This option is very safe and does not pose any danger to humankind. Rainbows do not leave any carbon footprint that can impact the environment.

Safe Fire Spells

If you are a novice in fire spells, there are certain steps you should follow as safety precautions. The easiest spell to perform is to simply light the fire then look into the flames. Think of the things you want to say or ask from the gods. Allow the flames to hypnotize you while you think deeply. When you cast the spells in this way, you can monitor the fire so that it does not get out of control.

Another spell involves a small fire that you place in the bowl. The flames usually burn fast, and you will be left with glowing embers that do not pose a lot of danger. You can add herbs to produce smoke which is not very dangerous. A successful spell does not necessarily mean that you must use flames. The heat produced from glowing embers can also help you achieve your goals if you perform the spells properly.

Get Fire Powers

Another effective way to perform fire spells safely is to get fire powers. Essentially, fire powers can allow you to control fire the way you want. You can also use the powers to create a fire. To get the power to control a fire, you must first acquire the skills through getting properly trained, which means that you must be committed and make an effort. Once you acquire the powers to control fire, you can safely manage different fires for yourself and those around you. These are magical powers you should obtain first to be able to control fire.

The good thing about being able to control fire is that you can apply the technique just like you do to control other elements, for example, water. For instance, you can control different things in your home or workplace to ensure safety for everyone. You can create the direction of water flow, and you can do the same with fire when you have appropriate powers. When you use it to control the element's spell, you are above the situation. However, it is crucial to start with small fires that are easy to control before you graduate to bonfires. Fire powers do not replace the need for standard fire safety in each situation, never leave a fire unattended.

Since time immemorial, fire spells have been used for various purposes in different places. While the practice of using fire to cast spells is common, fire spells can be destructive, since they pose potential danger to people and property. As we have discussed in this chapter, there are different measures you can consider to perform fire spells as safely as possible. It is also essential to use the right tools and equipment to prevent hazards. Every time you perform fire spells, safety should be your number one number one priority.

Chapter 9: Pyromancy – Divination by Fire

When you hear of the word "pyromania" these days, it's usually used in reference to someone with a penchant for setting things on fire. However, divination by pyromancy has been around for hundreds of years, and it has often been used as a way to look into the future or to stretch the psychic's own capabilities. Steeped in history, as you will have read in a previous chapter—the ancient Norse and pagans had a wide range of gods dealing with fire, so, whether you are in the early stages of your journey into witchcraft or have devoted yourself to studying it for a long while, you will agree that there is something rather magical and mysterious about fire. This chapter will explore how divination is achieved with fireworks and provide a brief cultural overview of how they have been used over time.

What Is Pyromancy?

Essentially, the word builds from the original Greek "pyros," which means fire, and "manteia," which means divination. A "pyromaniac" usually has bad intentions and is not at all interested in exploring the art of divination. However, the core of the word is historically meant to refer to this fascinating practice, and its meaning has been diluted over time.

A basic form of pyromancy involves a diviner watching the flames and looking for different clues or signs to decipher. Historically, this has been accomplished through the fire of a burning sacrifice, a candle, or any other source of flame. The diviner then watches carefully to see the images that may appear to them.

A Troubled History

Pyromancy has had a troubled history, with many people not understanding what it is all about and therefore fearing it and its potential outcomes.

The "caveman" discovered fire, and since then, humanity has never been the same. This invaluable technical development helped to usher in the solution to some of the basic necessities needed for survival, and it also created a source of fascination. The importance of fire in prehistoric and ancient civilizations can never be underestimated. While most people these days will not consider fire to be at all technical, it is, within the history of technology, an important accomplishment. Therefore, it makes sense for civilizations to have been spell-bound by this mysterious combustion of heat and light. It was most likely the earliest form of divination in history.

In both Western and non-Western cultures and religions, fire has usually been associated with a god—or thought to be a god itself. It was also treated as though it were a living being, as though it ate, breathed, and even decayed as a human body would. Again, the connection is unsurprising when you think of how crucial fire is to humans, and for it to be treated as an element of nature—which, technically, it is—is unsurprising.

The earliest known fire rituals were found in Mesopotamia, Eurasia, and other areas where fire temples or altars were used. Zoroastrians were the most famous believers in the power of fire and believed it to be a holy spirit whose icon was used in many religious services.

While fire was often used in religious services, the history of its use has also been intertwined with unsavory and frightening practices. In fact, during the Renaissance, pyromancy was often referred to as a forbidden form of magic, and many witches were burned at the stake as a result of their powers of divination. In addition to pyromancy, palmistry was also banned since it was considered sinful especially once Christianity took hold in the West. Necromancy, in which people attempted to converse or conjure up the dead, was also frowned upon, as well as any art that sought to mess with any of the elements, such as hydromancy (which deals with water), aeromancy (air), or geomancy (soil rock, sand).

Alternative Approaches to Pyromancy

While pyromancy has been badly misused in the past, including allegedly in some rituals that burned people alive for the sake of divination, it would be unjust to say that these were the only techniques used throughout time. Fire has been used in other ways as an oracle for hundreds of years, and modern witches have very specific methods to safely use this element to improve the lives of others. This section will outline how flames can be read and will help you to develop different techniques to enhance your understanding of pyromancy.

Alomancy

Alomancy is one of the earlier forms of divination, and it entails the diviner throwing salt crystals into the air and then seeing the pattern which is formed when they land. The diviner then interprets these patterns and even forms a sort of solution from the residue as it evaporates in a bowl or container. A more popular form of alomancy involves throwing these crystals into the fire, as opposed to the air, and interpreting the ways in which the flames evolve and take shape.

Salt is one of the compounds that is deeply tied to human history and has been part of our evolution in countless ways. Historically it has been used to denote luck, and even individuals who are merely superstitious and not at all interested in magic use salt. For example, a bit of salt is often thrown over the shoulder to ward off evil spirits and to maintain good luck.

Similarly, salt also culturally denotes falling into any kind of misfortune—such as when a salt cellar is upended or when a biblical figure is turned into a pillar of salt, as in the tale of Sodom and Gomorrah.

Geomancy

Another ancient practice, geomancy, is a method of divination centering on reading and interpreting markings on the ground. Historically it has also been used as a way to explore how handfuls of soil or sand land on the ground when someone tosses them into the air. It is sometimes a method of interpreting seemingly random markings and divining important signs and symbols in the landscapes. Similar to alomancy, this art can be combined with fire, as the diviner interprets flames and smoke patterns.

Ritual Cleansing

Apart from ancient magic, and with all the study that has gone into the significance of ancient techniques, we now know that fire was used in a number of ceremonial rituals. A ritual cleansing comes from a dark history of witchcraft, which is feared by a lot of superstitious people, cultures, and sects. In actuality, this type of ritual was used to get rid of hardship, but would, nowadays, be seen as cruel because people or animals who were "cursed" as being the cause of disharmony or the source of the devil's work were thrown into burning pyres during a ritual cleansing. One vital detail that is often left out is that those who made these sacrifices weren't traditionally evil witches. Some of these ceremonies were conducted by priests, members of the monarchy, shamans, and so on. Sometimes, the connections to "religion," "magic," or "dark arts" were removed from the equation, and ritual cleansings were performed by various tribes as a means to rid themselves of their enemies. Additionally, they were performed in times of war, drought, and famine or in light of other pandemics and natural disasters. Animals were often sacrificed to appease the gods, and the remaining carcass was often scanned for clues as to whether or not the sacrifice was accepted. Burn patterns, how much of the fire ate away at the corpse, or if the bones were cracked, were all indications meant to symbolise something to those performing the cleansing.

These days, ritual cleansings have come to mean something else entirely. In general, pyromancy is no longer considered to be a popular form of divination or magic. Few people practice it, given its long history as being thought of as something deeply unpleasant. Nevertheless, cleansing rituals have come to the fore lately and are rather popular amongst witches. The next section of this chapter will cover various ways in which ritual cleansings and other forms of pyromancy have been adapted for contemporary life.

Practical Forms of Pyromancy

Divination with fire is less known, and in some quarters, still remains shrouded in mystery. For those who are familiar with the practice, it can be difficult to shake off century-long negative connotations. However, at its very core, pyromancy is not very different from using a crystal ball or mirror or even water gazing. True, it may be a bit more difficult to learn, but mastering it can help you to better understand your own capabilities. Your senses and ability to see, hear, taste, touch, and smell will be carried to another level entirely, allowing you to become more grounded in spiritual ways.

One roadblock many people encounter when thinking about pyromancy is the fact that setting fire to something is impractical, not to mention dangerous. As a disclaimer, we would urge anyone curious to learn more about pyromancy to start small with candles, for example. Remember, safety must come first, and the flame is dangerous, so don't leave it unattended.

For those living in heavily populated urban areas, open fires have to be controlled, which makes learning the practice deeply impractical. Likewise, for those living in wide-open spaces, with nearby forests, fires can be dangerous. Wildfires sometimes happen naturally, but they can also be man-made disasters created by a reckless individual experimenting out in the open. Divination is about helping yourself and others, and it should never lead to harming the environment or people, which is why we suggest candles.

To try this, it is recommended that you first take the time to meditate and center yourself. Quieten your mind, and focus on cultivating the senses. Then, burn some incense and cast a circle of protection. Always light white candles for this exercise; never use one that is colored or is a strange shape. It should be unscented—you are doing this exercise to help sharpen the senses, so you will need a candle that is neutral. Also, stay away from windows or any place where there is a breeze, since that can cause you to misread the direction of the flames and what it is trying to tell you. Then, begin to focus your gaze on the flame. Begin to relax and concentrate more and more on the flame so that eventually, you are able to see the flame without looking at it directly. This may seem difficult, but give yourself a chance to look at the flame differently and notice whether it is beginning to change color, change in size, or flutter quickly as though the candle will be blown out any second. As you do this exercise, make a note of the different things you are perceiving and whether or not you are beginning to feel any different.

Eventually, you will snap out of it on your own since you've managed a form of self-hypnosis by gazing steadily at the flame and its aura. Do not be disheartened if it doesn't work the first few times you try. It probably just means you have tried too hard. When you start the practice of fire divination, it is important to not have too many expectations and to go in with an open mind. You cannot go in looking for answers or anything specific beyond simply allowing your mind to expand and thinking about whatever possibilities come into it without dreaming them up.

Also, for this kind of work to succeed, you need to prepare yourself well beforehand. For this reason, meditation and forming a protective circle around yourself is incredibly important. Some people have reported that being able to do this work well has led to a spirit guide coming through to help them as they perform the fire divination. At other times, you may not receive a major revelation of any kind, but rather, you may feel that you are on a higher plane and able to receive information in a powerful, completely undiluted manner. It ultimately depends on how much you practice this form of divination and how well you are able to harness your other spiritual capabilities in general.

In a more advanced stage of fire divination, you can slowly begin to ask questions. In this case, it is recommended that you begin slowly, without asking overly complicated questions that may be difficult for you to receive an answer for, thus breaking your concentration. You can start by asking "yes" and "no" questions until you become more confident about your ability to communicate via fire. Divination through candlelight is a deeply spiritual practice, and while it can take some time to become an expert, it is most certainly a skill worth learning.

Cleansing rituals were mentioned earlier in this book but in the context of historically dangerous and dark practices. Now, cleansing rituals have an entirely different meaning and technique, which many modern witches or spiritual individuals can safely incorporate into their daily lives. You will be using fire, of course, but in a slightly less dramatic fashion.

To perform a cleansing ritual, you need a cinnamon stick or a crystal—some prefer citrine or clear quartz, others amethyst, so choose the one that speaks to you most. You also need a candle, and paper and pen. Your candle should always be of neutral scent and color.

Before starting, write down on the paper the negative forces or feelings in your life that you'd like to burn away. Then, fold it and place it in front of you. Commence by lighting the candle and then set the cinnamon stick aflame. Use the smoke to trace lines around your body, over your head, and around your arms. The smoke may peter out every once in a while, and that's fine. Simply light it again from the candle.

After you have carefully circled the length of your body with the cinnamon stick, set it aside. Then, close your eyes and calmly visualize the flame of the candle, trying to quieten your mind. Breathe in and out, and take deep breaths into the belly, and release them slowly. Now, visualize letting go of the negative energy or memories of the person who hurt you. Focus on that visual, and release it into the air over and over again until you feel calm, and the action feels concrete. Then, take the piece of paper, and burn it with the candle flame. You've done it—this is one way in which pyromancy can be tangibly applied to our world.

Divination is a complicated art with a long history. Given how vital fire is to humanity, it makes sense for it to be one of the elements of strong magic and practicing psychic powers. Working with fire—albeit in a limited capacity with candles—can make you feel closer to the spiritual world, as well as with yourself. It is an eye-opening practice to look into, and you will learn a lot about yourself in the process.

Chapter 10: Your Own Fire Magic Ritual

Rituals have always been a significant aspect of human lives; whether they signify a specific religion or religious practice or are used for personal spiritual purposes, they can help us safely transcend the terrestrial realm and return again.

Fire has always been a powerful symbol in life and spirituality, as well. For instance, as you read in earlier chapters, in Hinduism, fire is used in various rituals, serving as a symbol and a connection to the Hindu gods. To them, fire can be both the destroyer and the creator of life, and it is an eminent concept in their practices. They have five sacred elements, of which fire is one. It is an essential everlasting symbol to sacred Hindu ceremonies.

Fire is the essence of life and is present in everything we do. Our life is fueled by the existence of fire, whether it is derived from the energy of the Sun or even the power of love. Fruit and vegetables need sunlight to grow and ripen, thus, in essence, feeding us condensed fire.

Whether you're new to the world of witchcraft or have been practicing it for a while now, it comes as no surprise that you'd be interested in giving fire magic rituals a go. Besides the fact that it sounds like a cool thing to do, mastering fire rituals can be very healing in terms of spirituality and energy, which takes the sting out of preconceived ideas that any ritual, ancient or modern, is the work of evil forces.

This chapter offers several full rituals dedicated to the fire element. You will find a step-by-step guide that lists the materials you'll need and how the ritual is to be performed. You'll also find out how to create and perform your own typical Wiccan ritual. Lastly, you'll come across a few safety disclaimers that ensure that you carry out the ritual as safely as possible.

Fire Rituals

Fire, by its very nature—ephemeral and colorful—is a very significant element when it comes to the concept of loss and new beginnings. The following are a few examples of rituals and spells that use fire to help you start over, rekindle your passion and drive, and make your way toward a promising future.

Cord-Cutting Ritual

Sometimes we meet people or find ourselves in places that are malevolent and hold us back. Keeping these toxic factors in our lives blocks better things from coming in. Cord-cutting rituals are typically used to help people cut ties with significant harmful others and leave relationships behind. However, they can also be used to let go of traumatic events or unwanted jobs.

Before preparing and performing this ritual, you must be very aware of the consequences. You must make sure that this is what you really want because once the ties are cut, the ritual can't be undone. The role of fire in this ritual is to burn all your connections to those elements you want to break away from.

Materials:

- A black or white candle.
- A lighter or matches.
- A candle holder.
- One 9-inch black string.
- A picture of yourself along with a picture of the person, place, job, or thing you want to cut ties with. (If you don't have pictures, get a piece of paper to write names.)
- Dried yarrow flowers (optional).
- Olive oil or other anointing oil (optional).

Ritual:

If you choose to use olive oil and the dried yarrow flowers, start by decorating the candle with them. While yarrow is not vital, it can help boost the spell's effects. This is because way back in pagan history, yarrow was associated with setting boundaries and cutting ties. Your second move is to tie one end of the string to each piece of rolled-up paper or picture. The string is nine inches long, as nine is the number of power and magic, giving your spell credence. Light the candle and visualize your desired future. Think of being happy, whole, and free of past traumas, hurts, or oppression. Whenever you feel ready, cut the cord that holds both photos and papers using the candle flame, while visualizing your goal. Inhale deeply and breathe out any emotions, tension, or feelings. Meditate on the future as the candle burns down.

Attraction Spell

When the word "witchcraft" comes up, most people think about love spells and curses. However, these are the most inaccurate stereotypes dreamed up by Hollywood and social media. Nothing can force a person to fall in love—not even magic. However, what is possible and what someone can do is attract a person to them. This can be done by making themselves more desirable. The "Attraction Spell" is used to draw people in and attract them. You can use this spell platonically to attract a friendship or romantically, attracting a lover. If you're not looking for someone new, you can use it to attract your dream job!

Materials:

- A pen.
- Two paper strips.
- A lighter or matches.
- A fireproof bowl.
- Wax.
- Orange blossom or orange zest.
- A spell bottle.

Spell:

On the first strip of paper, start by writing your goal or whatever you want to attract, using positive language, and having a clear intention that must be obvious in how you say the words. Make sure not to use the word "don't." Don't write what you don't want. Instead, write down the things you *do* want as if they are already yours. For instance, if you want to attract your dream job, write down "I have my dream job." On the second strip of paper, write down the object you want to attract. You can be as imprecise or specific as you want. For instance, if you want a specific person or job position, write their name or the job title at the desired place. If you want to attract love or a job in general, you can write what you desire in a person or the job. When you've done this, write your name over the object you want to attract. Place the orange zest or orange blossom in a bowl, insert both papers in, and burn. Put the ashes of the paper in a spell bottle and then use wax to seal it. Store the bottle in a safe place. If later on, you decide that you no longer want to attract that object, break the seal, and allow the ashes to fly into the wind.

Carnelian Strength Charm

Fire has always been linked to strength and passion. It is the perfect charm for when you're looking for the strength and courage you need to get things done. It can help you push forward regardless of anything that comes your way.

Materials:

- Jewelry wire.
- Carnelian.

Charm:

Around noon, when the sun is at its highest point, take your carnelian and cleanse it, then charge it up in the sunlight. Though, be careful not to leave it exposed to sunlight for more than an hour as it will begin to fade. Use jewelry wire to wrap around the carnelian once it's charged with sunlight. Recite the words "Carnelian, strong and proud, give me the strength to face the future with courage. Bring me the strength to face the unknown and the will to demand change. Help me remove all barriers to bring me happiness and good fortune." (*Elemental Magic: Fire Spells and Rituals*, 2020). As you make your pendant or keychain, you will begin to feel like you can take on the world.

Unblocking Spell

We sometimes tend to feel like something is holding us back, especially when it's time to get moving and get things done. Whether it's anger, doubt, or fear, blockage comes in endless forms. However, using fire to burn all these obstructions down can help clear your path. Following this spell up with a bath can help ensure that you're stripped away of any residual negative energies.

Materials:

- Whole cloves.
- A white candle.

Spell:

Visualize your doubts, fears, anger, or frustrations while holding the white candle. Use the whole cloves to decorate your candle, and then light it up. Focus on how the candle feels and warms in your hands as you continue to visualize. Picture everything that you've envisioned vanishing away with the smoke as the candle burns. Take your cleansing bath and change into clean and comfortable clothes. This is a symbol of new beginnings.

Create Your Own

If you don't resonate with any of the above rituals, charms, or spells, you can create your own magic ritual to bring your desires to life.

Practicing a release or invocation ritual is among the most powerful tools when it comes to dealing with energy and manifestation. You may be surprised to learn that creating your own ritual is not as hard as you think. It is a fairly simple technique that can be easily mastered and practiced regularly. The number of possibilities will blow your mind.

Find Your Sacred Space

If you don't have an altar or a sacred space yet, you need to find one where you feel most comfortable. It can be anywhere—some people feel most at peace when working outside, while others feel at ease working in a dimly lit corner in their room. The key is to feel grounded and focused. Though, make sure that you have access to good ventilation wherever you decide to perform the ritual. You can bring all your feathers, candles, stones, and whatever else you want to include in your experience. The sky's the limit. You can even bring a witchy cauldron and use it as a burning bowl if you desire. You should make sure that the bowl can withstand the heat, since you will be burning ink and paper. If you plan on performing the ritual with others, make sure that you have enough space to do so.

Planning and Deciding

Start thinking about the intent and purpose of your ritual. What do you want to get out of it, and how do you want to feel after it's complete? Think about how you're feeling now and what you truly desire. This will help you determine the course and direction of your ritual. If others are joining in with your ritual, you need to plan who will lead each part of the ritual. This will ensure that everything goes as smoothly as possible and that no confusion happens.

Setting Intentions

The most important part of your ritual is the intention setting one. When you're thinking about your intentions, you have to be grounded, and your thoughts have to be clear. If you're not feeling your best or you think your judgment may be clouded, partaking in a meditative activity is your best bet. Go on a relaxing walk, do breathing exercises, or get on the yoga mat.

Make sure that your feet are planted on the ground, and focus on your breaths to ground yourself. Take in several deep breaths and visualize energy coming from the ground up with every breath you take. Once you believe you're all set, it's time to write down your intentions. Think about everything that no longer serves you. This can be an emotion, a situation, a person, or a job. These are all things you can release. You can write a letter to your higher power or the universe, a poem, or even a list. The most important thing is that you're honest, genuine, and open with what you choose to release.

Invocation

After you're done with setting your intentions, you need to write down a list of everything you want to invoke. Write it down in the present tense. For instance, start the list with the words "I invoke." What you invoke should be things, emotions, and situations that you want to acquire.

Cast Your Circle

If you will be performing your ritual with others, make sure that they have grounded themselves, set their intentions, and written down their invocations as well. After everyone is done, gather around and cast your circle.

Calling the Elements

Once settled, you need to call the elements to gather around in your space. You need to start at the East and move clockwise. It should go like this: east, air—south, fire—west, water—north, earth—all, spirit.

Portray the Deities

You should take a moment or a few moments to honor your deity or deities. If you're having trouble focusing your mind, you can use a sculpture or an image of the god or goddess. This can also be helpful when many people are present, ensuring that everyone is focused on the same image.

Visualization

Take your time to visualize and meditate on your goals before you cast your spell.

Burn and Release

Now that you have written down all that you want to release and invoke; gathered the elements; portrayed your deities; and visualized your intentions, it's time to burn and release. Begin by burning the list of things that you don't want in your life anymore. As this list burns, you can recite a message to your higher self, deities, or the universe. You should communicate that you no longer need to learn the lessons that these unwanted situations or emotions are meant to teach you. Vow to learn them in a different way if you haven't already.

Then, burn the list that includes the things you want to invoke. As it burns, you can recite another message to your higher self, deities, or the universe. Communicate that the desired emotions and situations are going to serve your best interest and that you intend to use them to move forward in life and become a better version of yourself.

Take several deep breaths and finish off by rubbing your hands together. This symbolizes letting go of the attachments to anything that you have just released. This applies to both the things you desire and the things you don't.

Ending the Ritual

Thank your deity or deities along with the elements. You should release the elements in the opposite order to that which you gathered them. Open your circle to let go of any residual energy. You can either do that while you release the elements or once you've done it. Ground yourself again and bring yourself to the present moment. You can write down your experience in a book of shadows after you're done and whenever you feel ready.

Disclaimers

- Avoid wearing loose or badly fitting clothing during the ritual to prevent it from catching on fire.

- Make sure not to leave any candles, incense, or charcoal embers burning if no one is around.

- Keep any candle or burning object away from flammable materials. You also need to make sure that no children or pets are around during the process.

- Make sure that the cauldron or bowl is fireproof.

Fire is a very powerful element. It draws a very thin line between creative and destructive energies. It's all fun and games until it gets out of control. We start fires in our homes to keep us warm. However, when we lose control over a fire, it could end up burning the entire place down.

Similarly, using fires in your rituals can be quite rewarding and exciting. It is a purifying element that can rid you of anything that no longer serves you. There's more to fire than just its physical combustion. It can reset your energy and cleanse your soul. It makes space for better and more positive things. Fire, and all that it offers, can help us thrive. However, incorrect and careless utilization of fire can result in devastating effects.

Conclusion

The primary focus of this book was to provide you with some new information on fire magic, as well as some of the historical background of fire as a magical element. This book is distinctive in that it tackles controversial issues related to the supernatural world. As you read through different chapters, you learned many things about fire magic that will make a difference in your life if you apply them.

Are you interested in understanding the history of fire? If yes, then this informative book is a must-read, since it is specially written to provide you with helpful details about fire magic basics. You have probably heard something about magic spells, and this may be an area of interest. However, performing different spells can be overwhelming if you are a beginner. With the appropriate knowledge about the purpose and significance of fire magic, you can easily learn what you want to know about this discipline.

People use fire magic in different circumstances. Other elements like witchcraft and spells exist, so you should know how to deal with them in real life. You can only achieve this if you have the right information about the magic world.

If you are interested in gaining expert tips in practical applications of spells, here they are in one easy-to-access place. *Fire Magic: Secrets of Witchcraft, Spells, Candle Burning Rituals, Norse Paganism, and Divination* is great for beginners and experienced fire magicians alike, since it provides a hands-on approach and instructions to help master various techniques quickly. With this book, you can learn different concepts about fire magic that you may wish to apply in your life. Additionally, the book is easy to understand, and you can follow the instructions without seeking guidance from an instructor. It is written in a step-by-step manner to help grasp everything you may need to know about fire magic.

Another reason why this book is good for beginners like you is that it comprises a host of pictures to keep you visually engaged. The images you find in the book tell different stories that aim to enlighten you about various components of fire spells. The pictures also provide easy-to-follow instructions to improve your practical skills if you want to experiment with fire magic.

It is important to remember safety when working with the element of fire. Whatever its purpose, fire can be dangerous. It can cause damage to property or bodily harm, but this book provides expert tips about how to use fire magic. The safety tips are outlined throughout the book and are designed to equip you with knowledge about different measures that should be taken to prevent danger when performing spells.

Fire Magic: Secrets of Witchcraft, Spells, Candle Burning Rituals, Norse Paganism, and Divination sets the record straight and dispels myths about the purpose and significance of this type of magic. Get your copy today and enjoy the secrets of witchcraft, candle burning rituals, spells, and Norse paganism.

Here's another book by Mari Silva that you might like

Your Free Gift (only available for a limited time)

Thanks for getting this book! If you want to learn more about various spirituality topics, then join Mari Silva's community and get a free guided meditation MP3 for awakening your third eye. This guided meditation mp3 is designed to open and strengthen ones third eye so you can experience a higher state of consciousness. Simply visit the link below the image to get started.

https://spiritualityspot.com/meditation

References

Fire Element. (n.d.). Retrieved from Complementary-therapists.com website:

http://www.complementary-therapists.com/five-element/fire.htm

Fire Element Symbolism & Meaning. (2016, May 29). Retrieved from Buildingbeautifulsouls.com website:

https://www.buildingbeautifulsouls.com/symbols-meanings/five-elements-symbolic-meaning/fire-element-symbolic-meaning

Greek Medicine: The Four Basic Qualities—Yin and Yang, Greek-Style. (n.d.). Retrieved from Greekmedicine.net website:

http://www.greekmedicine.net/b_p/Four_elements.html

Telesco, P., and Wise Witch. *The Elements in Magic and Witchcraft: Fire Symbolism, Meaning & Uses.* (2018, May 4). Retrieved from Witchcraftandwitches.com

website: https://witchcraftandwitches.com/witchcraft/the-elements-in-magic-and-witchcraft-fire-symbolism-meaning-uses

What Plants and Herbs Are Attributed to Fire? (n.d.). Retrieved from Groveandgrotto.com website:

https://www.groveandgrotto.com/blogs/articles/36713217-what-plants-and-herbs-are-attributed-to-fire

Avad, S. *Salamanders, Elemental of Fire.* (2017, September 18). Retrieved from

Aminoapps.com website:

https://aminoapps.com/c/mythfolklore/page/blog/salamanders-elemental-of-fire/1DgR_l0t6u0PGYG8garnMqNYRJ5JWGaMXJ

Brigid: Goddess of the Flame and of the Well. (n.d.). Retrieved from Wicca-spirituality.com

website: https://www.wicca-spirituality.com/brigid.html

Gay, M. *Phoenix, Mythical Bird—Occultopedia, the Occult and Unexplained Encyclopedia.*

(n.d.). Retrieved from Occultopedia.com website:

http://occultopedia.com/p/phoenix.htm

Gay, M. *Salamanders, Fire Spirits—Occultopedia, the Occult and Unexplained Encyclopedia.*

(n.d.). Retrieved from Occultopedia.com website:

https://www.occultopedia.com/s/salamander.htm

Paula. *Mythological Creatures of Fire.* (n.d.). Retrieved from Blogspot.com website:

https://testforbloggerandgadgets.blogspot.com/2014/02/mythological-creatures-of-fire-mythical.html

Reusser, K. *Hephaestus.* (2009). Mitchell Lane.

Wigington, P. *Brighid, the Hearth Goddess of Ireland.* (n.d.). Retrieved from Learnreligions.com website: https://www.learnreligions.com/brighid-hearth-goddess-of-ireland-2561958

Wigington, P. *The Magic and Folklore of Fire.* (n.d.). Retrieved from Learnreligions.com website: https://www.learnreligions.com/fire-element-folklore-and-legends-2561686

Mark, J. J. *Vesta—World History Encyclopedia.* (2009). Retrieved from Worldhistory.org

website: https://www.worldhistory.org/Vesta

Geller. *Vulcan.* (2017, April 9). Retrieved from Mythology.net website:

https://mythology.net/roman/roman-gods/vulcan

Hestia. (2014, September 19). Retrieved from Greekgodsandgoddesses.net website:

https://greekgodsandgoddesses.net/goddesses/hestia

Spring, S. *Dragons: The Magic & the Mysticism.* (2011, September 29). Retrieved from

HubPages.com website:

https://discover.hubpages.com/education/Dragons-The-Magic-The-Mysticism

Angelica. *Altar Setup and Upkeep.* (2019, May 12). Retrieved from Thelongship.net website:

https://www.thelongship.net/2019/05/12/altar-setup-and-upkeep

April. *Some Basic Altar Set Up Information.* (n.d.). Retrieved from Witchdigest.com website:

https://witchdigest.com/27337/some-basic-altar-set-up-information

Estrada, J. *How to Make Your Very Own Altar at Home.* (2021, April 30). Retrieved from

Cosmopolitan.com website:

https://www.cosmopolitan.com/lifestyle/a36302874/how-to-make-an-altar

Modern Traditional Witch, A. *The Element of Fire as an Altar in Witchcraft.* (2019, April 10).

Retrieved from Patheos.com website: https://www.patheos.com/blogs/tempest/2019/04/the-element-of-fire-as-an-altar-in-witchcraft.html

Netra. *Simple Altar Set Up for Beginners.* (2019, January 27). Retrieved from

Thebrownperfection.com website:

https://thebrownperfection.com/2019/01/27/simple-altar-set-up-for-beginners

Anderberg, J. *A Complete Guide to Home Fire Prevention and Safety.* (2013, November 8).

Retrieved from Artofmanliness.com website:

https://www.artofmanliness.com/lifestyle/homeownership/a-complete-guide-to-home-fire-prevention-and-safety

Calcite Meaning: Healing Properties & Everyday Uses. (n.d.). Retrieved from Tinyrituals.co website:

https://tinyrituals.co/blogs/tiny-rituals/calcite-meaning-healing-properties-everyday-uses

Carnelian Meaning: Healing Properties & Everyday Uses. (n.d.). Retrieved from Tinyrituals.co website: https://tinyrituals.co/blogs/tiny-rituals/carnelian-meaning-healing-properties

Crystals and Their Relation to the Elements. (n.d.). Retrieved from Sunnyray.org website: https://www.sunnyray.org/Crystals-elements.htm

Gemstone Information: Citrine Meaning and Properties—Fire Mountain Gems and Beads.

(n.d.). Retrieved from Firemountaingems.com website:

https://www.firemountaingems.com/resources/encyclobeadia/gem-notes/gemnotecitrine

Gemstone Information: Labradorite Meaning and Properties—Fire Mountain Gems and Beads.

(n.d.). Retrieved from Firemountaingems.com website:

https://www.firemountaingems.com/resources/encyclobeadia/gem-notes/gmstnprprtslbrd

Kyteler, E. (2019, June 28). *Herbs and Plants for Witchcraft: Fire Element Herbs*. Retrieved from Eclecticwitchcraft.com website: https://eclecticwitchcraft.com/fire-element-herbs

Mitchell, K. N. *Crystals + Fire Element Magic: Purification & Transformation*. (2019, July 21).

Retrieved from Krista-mitchell.com website:

https://www.krista-mitchell.com/blog/crystalsfireelement

Spessartine Meanings and Uses—Crystal Vaults. (2013, April 3). Retrieved from

Crystalvaults.com website: https://www.crystalvaults.com/crystal-encyclopedia/spessartine

Sunstone Meaning: Healing Properties & Everyday Uses. (n.d.). Retrieved from Tinyrituals.co website: https://tinyrituals.co/blogs/tiny-rituals/sunstone-meaning-healing-properties-everyday-uses

What Plants and Herbs Are Attributed to Fire? (n.d.). Retrieved from Groveandgrotto.com

website: https://www.groveandgrotto.com/blogs/articles/36713217-what-plants-and-herbs-are-attributed-to-fire

Elly, M. *Loki and Logi: Two Different Characters in Norse Myth*. (2019, November 12).

Retrieved from Bavipower.com website:

https://bavipower.com/blogs/bavipower-viking-blog/loki-and-logi-two-different-characters-in-norse-myth

Greenberg, M. *Where was Muspelheim?* (2020, November 3). Retrieved from

Mythologysource.com website: https://mythologysource.com/where-was-muspelheim

How Odin Sacrificed His Eye at Mimir's Well. (n.d.). Retrieved from Thevikingdragon.com website: https://thevikingdragon.com/blogs/news/how-odin-sacrificed-his-eye-at-mimirs-well

Jessica, S. *Muspelheim.* (2020, June 8). Retrieved from Vkngjewelry.com website:

https://blog.vkngjewelry.com/en/muspelheim

Logi: About Logi. (n.d.). Retrieved from Northernpaganism.org website:

http://www.northernpaganism.org/shrines/logi/about.html

The Significance of Fire in Norse Mythology. (n.d.). Retrieved from Scotdir.com website: http://scotdir.com/home/society-and-lifestyle/the-significance-of-fire-in-norse-mythology

Shop, L. *Candle Burning Magic (Colors and What They Mean).* (2012, May 21). Retrieved from

Luckshop.com website: https://blog.luckshop.com/candle-burning-magic-colors-mean

Magical Powers of Candles & Prayers. (n.d.). Retrieved from Blogspot.com website:

http://spiritmanjoseph.blogspot.com/2009/07/magical-powers-of-candles-prayers.html

Black Candle: Meaning and How Powerful it is for Prayers. (n.d.). Retrieved from

Pandagossips.com website: https://pandagossips.com/posts/1388

Burchell, C. *How to Perform a Candle Ritual.* (2019, February 8). Retrieved from

Tinyritual.com website: https://www.tinyritual.com/guide/candleritual

Wright, M. S. *Witchcraft: Beginner's Guide to Candle Magic.* (2014, August 21). Retrieved from

Exemplore.com website: https://exemplore.com/wicca-witchcraft/Witchcraft-Beginners-Guide-to-Candle-Magic

Twelve of the Most Dazzling Fire Festivals in the World. (n.d.). Retrieved from Everfest.com website: https://www.everfest.com/magazine/12-of-the-most-dazzling-fire-festivals-in-the-world

Festivals. (2017, July 15). Retrieved from Wordpress.com website: https://celticpaganism.wordpress.com/festivals

Kyle, V. *A Guide to the Biggest Fire Festivals in the World.* (2017, November 3). Retrieved

from Holidaytaxis.com website: https://www.holidaytaxis.com/blog/en/biggest-fire-festivals-in-the-world

The Wheel of the Year: The Calendar of Pagan Festivals Explained. (n.d.). Retrieved from

History.co.uk website: https://www.history.co.uk/articles/the-wheel-of-the-year-the-calendar-of-pagan-festivals-explained

Wigington, P. *What are Quarter Days and Cross-Quarter Days?* (n.d.). Retrieved from

Learnreligions.com website: https://www.learnreligions.com/quarter-days-and-cross-quarter-days-2562061

Ceridwen. *Fire Spells: Introductory Elemental Magic.* (2019, March 18). Craftofwicca.com

website: https://craftofwicca.com/fire-spells-elemental-magic

Eight Protection Rules Every Witch Should Know. (2019, March 12). Retrieved from

Spells8.com website: https://spells8.com/lessons/protection-safety-casting-spells

Fire Spells—Ancient, Primal Magic. (n.d.). Retrieved from Magic-spells-and-potions.com https://magic-spells-and-potions.com/fire_spells_ancient_primal_magic.htm

Voodoo and Magic: Using Fire Spells to Control a Fire. (2019, April 21). Retrieved from Voodoo-and-Magic.com website: https://www.voodoo-and-magic.com/fire-spells

Shirley Twofeathers. *Fire Magick.* (n.d.). Retrieved from Shirleytwofeathers.com website: https://shirleytwofeathers.com/The_Blog/bookofshadows/category/fire-magick

Elemental Magic: Tools of Fire. (2020, July 13). Retrieved from Flyingthehedge.com website: https://www.flyingthehedge.com/2020/07/elemental-series-tools-of-fire.html

Hamilton-Parker, C. *Pyromancy: Pyromancer's Guide to Fire Divination.* (2012, June 15). Retrieved from Psychics.co.uk website: https://psychics.co.uk/blog/pyromancy

Pyromancy: Fire Divination Guide. (2021, May 29). Retrieved from Terravara.com website: https://www.terravara.com/pyromancy-fire-divination

Wigington, P. *Fire Scrying Ritual.* (n.d.). Retrieved from Learnreligions.com website: https://www.learnreligions.com/fire-scrying-ritual-2561755

Elemental Magic: Fire Spells and Rituals. (2020, July 27). Retrieved from Flyingthehedge.com website: https://www.flyingthehedge.com/2020/07/elemental-magic-fire-spells-and-rituals.html

Hopkins, J. *How to Create and Use a Ritual Fire in Your Magic.* (n.d.). Retrieved from

Thetravelingwitch.com website:

https://thetravelingwitch.com/blog/how-to-create-and-use-a-ritual-fire-in-your-magic

Pickett, L. *How to Do a Burning Ritual (Release/Invocation).* (2013, October 4). Retrieved from

Moonandmanifest.com website: https://moonandmanifest.com/burning-ritual

Significance of Fire in Rituals. (2015, October 11). Retrieved from Dailyexcelsior.com website:

https://www.dailyexcelsior.com/significance-of-fire-in-rituals